THE 30-MINUTE MEDITERRANEAN DIET FOR TWO

SOFIA RUSSO

TABLE OF CONTENT

INTRODUCTION

This book is about learning how to live a healthy lifestyle through eating. Researchers have shown that the Mediterranean diet is one of the most nutritious diets globally because those who follow it live healthier, longer lives, free from the influence of chronic diseases. Diseases relating to the heart are the most prevalent across the globe. If we consider adopting this diet as a preventative strategy in our daily lives, the rate of cardiac illnesses may drop. Furthermore, it is possible to reduce your excess body weight by many kilograms through the Mediterranean diet. It is a safe diet for individuals of all ages after childhood.

This diet has another remarkable effect on the happiness and health of human beings, and that is better cognition. Consuming large amounts of foods rich in antioxidants and amino acids helps protect your mental health. Antioxidants through fruits and vegetables (e.g., citrus fruits and bell peppers) help clear the toxins out from your cells. These toxins are mainly composed of the residue left behind by proteins from animal sources. Amino acids that make proteins are the primary fuel for developing brain cells and agents of healthy mental functioning.

This diet is a complete package for anyone who desires a healthy body and mind. Start fighting infections and minor everyday health problems to resist significant diseases like diabetes and cancers. You may find this diet in traditional and contemporary contexts: you may see someone including only raw foods on the plate, while others might add lamb chops. Both ways will work for you as long as you correctly follow the diet guidelines. Key points to remember are: be as simple as possible, be as creative as possible when combining foods from different food groups, and feel satisfied.

HEALTH BENEFITS OF THE MEDITERRANEAN DIET

The Mediterranean diet lifestyle is one of the healthiest diets in the world. In fact, it is one of the most researched and extensively acclaimed diets, as proven by a substantial amount of scientific studies conducted over the past sixty years.

The following are just some of the amazing health benefits offered by this way of eating. Numerous studies have shown that following the Mediterranean diet has the following benefits:

- **Improved symptoms of sleep apnea**
- Improved mental and physical health
- **Improvement in bone and teeth health**
- Lower risk for some types of cancer
- **Slower decline of brain health due to aging, thus lower risk of Alzheimer's disease**
- Prevention of Parkinson's disease
- **Reduced inflammation and increased flowing levels of antioxidants**
- Lower risk of developing type two diabetes
- **Lower chances of developing depression**
- Lower risk of developing heart diseasese
- **Lower risk of having a heart attack or stroke**
- Better management of blood-sugar levels in people diagnosed with type two diabete

The Mediterranean diet in itself tends to induce weight loss, because the portion sizes of certain food types are limited, and the meals are generally savored and enjoyed, not consumed hastily.

HOW TO START

The Mediterranean lifestyle is an easy way to get back on track with your healthy eating habits. It has been found that people who live in this region have lower obesity, heart disease, and diabetes rates than the average person. The Mediterranean diet is an excellent choice for anyone looking to get healthier, lower cholesterol levels, and lose weight.

Now that you have been introduced to the wonders of a Mediterranean diet, it is time to show you how easy and delicious transitioning into this lifestyle can be. I'll walk you through a five-step guide to making the transition from your old ways with healthy eating habits, so come with me on an exciting journey to better health.

I have compiled five steps below for your ease in transitioning to the Mediterranean diet.

Use Olive Oil

It is necessary to substitute other fats with olive oil if you want the benefits of the Mediterranean diet. Olive oil is central to this type of diet, and it contains good fats. But, if you do not replace other types of fat with olive oil, you will not get those benefits.

Eat Vegetables as the Main Dish

One of the main features that set the Mediterranean Diet apart from most other diets is its high consumption of vegetables. Greeks consume almost a pound per day, which can be seen in their cooking techniques, such as sautéed green beans with olive oil or tomato sauce.

Cook Simple Mediterranean Meals

The Mediterranean diet is a refreshing change from the Western standard. It consists of real food that can make your life happier and healthier, like omelets with fresh vegetables or grilled fish topped with tomatoes.
You might not have to cook from scratch every day, but learning 2-3 essential dishes will help you in the long run.

Try Going Vegan One Day A Week

It may have been that the Greeks' diet was so healthy because they abstained from animal products for roughly half of their year. This would make sense as a religious practice and potentially an important factor in why this population had much better health than others due to less meat consumption and more plant-based foods.

Do Not Add Meat to Everything

Many people see vegetables on the recommendation list, but what does meat add to a diet? Studies show that reducing your red and white meats intake will have better health benefits. Try these guidelines: one serving of lean beef once per week | three servings of chicken weekly, one every two days, with fish as an alternative for those who do not like seafood.

TRICKS FOR SUCCESS IN THE MEDITERRANEAN DIET

The Mediterranean Diet is a lifestyle choice that has many health benefits, and it is easy to maintain as well. First, you must know what foods are allowed on the Mediterranean diet.

On a typical day of eating on the Mediterranean Diet, your plate would be filled with fruits and vegetables firstly, then an appropriate amount of meat or fish, followed by starchy carbs like whole-grain rice or pasta. Alongside these three food groups, there will also be plenty of olive oil-based dressings and sauces used liberally throughout meals. This gives you an idea about how varied your options can be when following this way of life. While many people dive right into this new way of eating without planning or understanding the ins and outs of what they should be doing to achieve their goals, there are some tricks you can use to make your journey easier. That is precisely what this chapter is going to be about | it will discuss some tricks for ensuring your success in adapting to the Mediterranean diet.

Eat-In A Way That Is Mindful and Moderate
The Mediterranean Diet is different from other eating plans because it allows you to have some foods high in fat while still being healthy. Eating this way can also make your brain more beneficial and help reduce risk factors for heart disease. It is not about starving yourself or cutting out entire food groups. Instead, eat moderately without going overboard on certain foods, especially sweets.

Finding fruits and vegetables
If you do not usually eat much fresh produce, it might be hard to start eating an apple or broccoli. But there are some vegetables that most people like: gateway vegetables or fruits. You just need to find the one that works for you and start eating that every day. And then, you can gradually go on to other healthy Mediterranean foods like tomatoes, cucumbers, green peppers, and carrots. It might take a year or more before the change happens, but it is worth it because you will feel better.

Include Signature Ingredients
Tasty food is the best way to make your diet enjoyable. The Mediterranean diet is popular because it has ingredients that everyone likes. You can find recipes from around the Mediterranean that use the same signature ingredients. Such as olive oil, whole grains, and vegetables. They use a limited amount of fish, red meat, and chicken for protein.

Incorporate Weight Loss Components
The Mediterranean diet does not always have to be for weight loss, but it can be. For this, first, you need to restrict your portions and calories to lose some weight. Simple kitchen tools will help with measuring spoons and a food scale. Apps will help you figure out how many of the right foods you should eat in a day. It might even make it easier for you to tailor healthy Mediterranean-style meals.

MEDITERRANEAN RECIPES

BREAKFAST

Greek Yogurt Pancakes

Preparation Time: 10 minutes
Cooking Time: 5 minutes
Total Time: 15 minutes

- 1 cup all-purpose flour
- 2 teaspoons vanilla extract
- 1 cup whole-wheat flour
- 1/4 teaspoon salt
- 1 Tablespoon sugar
- 1 1/2 cups unsweetened almond milk
- 2 large eggs
- 4 teaspoons baking powder
- Maple syrup, for serving
- 1/2 cup 2% Greek yogurt Fruit, for serving

1. First, you will have to pour the yogurt into a bowl and mix it well.
2. Next, you'll need to add the egg whites and combine them well.
3. Take another bowl and pour the dry mixture into the wet mixture. Stir to combine. The batter will be very thick.
4. Pour the batter onto the oiled skillet and heat over medium-high. You need to form 4 large pancakes.
5. Flip the pancakes when they begin to bubble a bit on the surface. Cook until golden brown on both sides.

Per Serving:
Calories: 166; Fat: 5g; Carbs: 52g; Protein: 14g

Low-Carb Baked Eggs With Avocado And Feta

Preparation Time: 10 minutes
Cooking Time: 15 minutes
Total Time: 25 minutes

- 1 avocado
- 4 eggs
- 2-3 tbsp crumbled feta cheese
- Non-stick cooking spray
- Pepper and salt to taste

1. Preheat oven to 400 degrees F.
2. After that, when the oven is at temperature, place the dishes to be gratinated directly on the baking sheet.
3. Let the dishes warm up in the oven for 8 minutes.
4. Crack an egg into each ramekin.
5. Allow the avocado and eggs to cool to room temperature for at least 10 minutes. Next, peel the avocado and cut each half into 6-8 slices.
6. You will have to take the dishes out of the oven and spray them with non-stick spray.
7. Next, you will have to put all the sliced avocados in the dishes and pour two eggs onto each plate. Add pepper and salt to taste and sprinkle with feta cheese.
8. Lastly, bake until the egg whites are set and the yolks are done to your liking. Serve hot.

Per Serving:
Calories: 280; Fat: 23.5g; Carbs: 9.3g; Protein: 11.3g

Spinach And Egg Breakfast Wraps

Preparation Time: 10 minutes
Cooking Time: 7 minutes
Total Time: 17 minutes

- 1 tablespoon olive oil
- ¼ cup minced onion
- 3 to 4 tablespoons minced sun-dried tomatoes in olive oil and herbs
- 3 large eggs, whisked
- 1½ cups packed baby spinach
- 1 ounce (28 g) crumbled feta cheese
- Salt, to taste
- 2 (8-inch) whole-wheat tortillas

1. Pour the oil into a large frying skillet over medium heat.
2. Sauté the onion and tomatoes for about 3 minutes, occasionally stirring, until softened.
3. Reduce the heat to medium. Add the whisked eggs and stir-fry for 1 to 2 minutes.
4. Stir in the baby spinach and scatter with the crumbled feta cheese. Season as needed with salt.
5. Remove the egg mixture from the heat to a plate. Set aside.
6. Working in batches, place 2 tortillas on a microwave-safe dish and heat for about 20 seconds

7. Spread half of the egg mixture on each tortilla. Fold in half and roll up, then serve.

Per Serving
Calories: 434; fat: 28.1g; carbs: 30.8g; protein: 17.2g

Almond Banana Pancakes

Preparation Time: 10 minutes
Cooking Time: 10 minutes
Total Time: 20 minutes

- ¼ cup almond flour
- ½ teaspoon ground cinnamon
- 3 eggs
- 1 banana, mashed
- 1 tablespoon almond butter
- 1 teaspoon vanilla extract
- 1 teaspoon olive oil
- Sliced banana to serve

1. Mix the eggs in a bowl until they become fluffy.
2. In another bowl, mash the banana using a fork and add it to the egg mixture. Add the vanilla, almond butter, cinnamon and almond flour.
3. Mix into a smooth batter.
4. Heat the olive oil in a skillet.
5. Add one tablespoon of batter and fry on both sides.
6. Continue doing these steps until you have finished all the batter.

7. Add some sliced banana on the top before serving.

Per Serving:

Calories: 306; Carbs: 3.6g; Fat: 26g; Protein: 14.4g

Parmesan Omelet

Preparation time: 5 minutes
Cooking time: 10 minutes
Total Time: 15 minutes

- 1 tablespoon cream cheese
- 2 eggs, beaten
- ¼ teaspoon paprika
- ½ teaspoon dried oregano
- ¼ teaspoon dried dill
- 1 oz Parmesan, grated
- 1 teaspoon coconut oil

1. Mix up together cream cheese with eggs, dried oregano, and dill.
2. Place coconut oil in the pan and heat it.
3. Then pour the egg mixture into the pan and flatten it.
4. Add grated Parmesan and cover with a lid.
5. Cook omelet for 10 minutes over low heat.
6. Transfer the omelet to the serving plate and sprinkle with paprika.

Per Serving:

Calories: 148; fat: 11.5g; carbs: 1.4g; protein: 10.6g

Avocado Milk Shake

Preparation Time: 10 minutes
Cooking Time: 0 minutes

- 1 avocado, peeled, pitted
- 2 tablespoons of liquid honey
- ½ teaspoon vanilla extract
- ½ cup heavy cream
- 1 cup milk
- 1/3 cup ice cubes

1. Place the cut avocado in the food processor.
2. Add heavy cream, honey, ice cubes, vanilla extract and milk.
3. Blend the mixture until it is smooth.
4. Serve in glasses.

Per Serving:

Calories: 291g; fat: 22.1g; carbs: 22g; protein: 4.4g

Cauliflower Fritters

Preparation time: 10 minutes
Cooking time: 10 minutes
Total Time: 20 minutes

- 1 cup cauliflower, shredded
- 1 egg, beaten
- 1 tablespoon wheat flour, whole grain
- 1 oz Parmesan, grated
- ½ teaspoon ground black pepper
- 1 tablespoon canola oil

1. In a mixing bowl, mix up together the egg and shredded cauliflower.
2. Add wheat flour, grated ground black pepper and Parmesan.
3. Stir the mixture until it is homogenous and smooth.
4. Pour canola oil into the pan and bring it to a boil.
5. From the cauliflower mixture, make the fritters with the help of your fingertips.
6. Fry the fritters for 3 minutes from each side over medium-high heat.

Per Serving:
Calories: 167; fat: 12.3g; carbs: 6.7g; protein: 8.8g

Cocoa Oatmeal

Preparation time: 10 minutes
Cooking time: 15 minutes
Total Time: 25 minutes

- 1 ½ cup oatmeal
- 1 tablespoon cocoa powder
- ½ cup heavy cream
- ¼ cup of water
- 1 teaspoon vanilla extract
- 1 tablespoon butter
- 2 tablespoons Splenda

1. Mix oatmeal with cocoa powder and Splenda.
2. Transfer the mixture to the saucepan.
3. Add water, vanilla extract and heavy cream. Stir it with the help of the fork.
4. Cover and cook it for 10-15 minutes over medium-low heat.
5. Stir in the butter and remove the cocoa-baked oatmeal from the heat.

Per Serving:
Calories: 230; fat: 10.6g; carbs: 28.1g; protein: 4.6g

Breakfast Green Smoothie

Preparation Time: 7 minutes
Cooking Time: 0 minutes

- 2 cups spinach
- 2 cups kale
- 1 cup bok choy
- 1 ½ cup organic almond milk
- 1 tablespoon almonds, chopped
- ½ cup of water

1. Put all ingredients in the blender and blend until you get a smooth mixture.
2. Pour the smoothie into the serving glasses.
3. Add ice cubes if desired.

Per Serving:
Calories 107; fat: 3.6g; carbs: 15.5g; protein: 4.8g

Creamy Parsley Soufflé

Preparation Time: 10 minutes

Cooking Time: 10 minutes
Total Time: 20 minutes

- 2 fresh red chili peppers, chopped
- Salt, to taste
- 4 eggs
- 4 tablespoons light cream
- 2 tablespoons fresh parsley, chopped

1. Preheat the oven, set to 375 F and grease 2 soufflé dishes.
2. Combine all the ingredients in a bowl and mix well.
3. Put the mixture into the prepared soufflé dishes and transfer to the oven.
4. Bake for about 6 minutes and serve immediately.
5. You can refrigerate this creamy parsley soufflé in foil-lined ramekins for meal prep for about 2-3 days.

Per Serving:
Calories: 108; Fat: 9g; Carbs: 1.1g; Protein: 6g

Vanilla Pancakes

Preparation Time: 10 minutes
Cooking Time: 5 minutes
Total time: 15 minutes

- 6 ounces plain yogurt
- ½ cup whole-grain flour
- 1 egg, beaten
- 1 teaspoon vanilla extract
- 1 teaspoon baking powder

1. Heat non-stick frying pan well.
2. Meanwhile, mix up all ingredients together.
3. Pour the mixture into the skillet in the shape of the pancakes.
4. Cook them for 1 minute per side.

Per Serving:
Calories: 202; Carbs: 29.4g; Fat: 3.8g; Protein: 11.7g

Scrambled Eggs

Preparation Time: 5 minutes
Cooking Time: 10 minutes
Total Time: 15 minutes

- 4 cherry tomatoes, quartered
- ½ of medium yellow bell pepper, cored, diced
- 1 medium spring onion, sliced
- 1 tablespoon parsley
- ½ tablespoon capers
- ¼ teaspoon ground black pepper
- ¼ teaspoon salt
- ¼ teaspoon dried oregano
- 2 large eggs, at room temperature

1 Take a medium skillet, place over medium heat, add oil, and when hot, add bell pepper, onion and cook for 3 minutes until softened
2 Add tomatoes and capers, then cook for 1 minute, stirring occasionally.

3 Crack eggs into the pan, stir the eggs constantly and cook for 3 to 4 minutes until eggs have scrambled to the desired level.
4 Then add oregano, salt, and black pepper, stir until well combined, and cook for 1 minute and eggs are fully cooked.
5 Divide the scrambled eggs evenly between two plates, sprinkle with parsley and serve.

Per Serving
Calories: 249; Fat: 17g; Sat. Fat: 3.8g; Carbs: 13.3g; Protein: 13.5g

Mini Omelette

Preparation Time: 5 minutes
Cooking Time: 20 minutes
Total Time: 25 minutes

- 4 tablespoons chopped mixed vegetables
- ¼ teaspoon salt
- ¼ teaspoon ground black pepper
- ¼ teaspoon Italian seasoning
- 2 large eggs, at room temperature
- 2 tablespoons half and half, low-fat
- 2 tablespoons shredded cheddar cheese, low-fat

1. Switch on the oven, set it to 177 degrees C or 350 degrees F, and let it preheat.
2. Meanwhile, take a baking tray, place two ramekins on it, spray the ramekins with

cooking spray to grease them, and set them aside until required.

3. Take a medium mixing bowl, crack eggs in it, add half and half, and whisk until fluffy.
4. Then add salt, black pepper, Italian seasoning, and cheese, and stir until combined.
5. Add mixed vegetables into the bowl, fold until well mixed, and then spoon the mixture evenly into the prepared ramekins.
6. Place the baking tray containing prepared ramekins into the oven and bake for 20 minutes, or until firm and the top turns golden brown.
7. When done, let the omelet muffins cool down at room temperature for 5 minutes, and then serve.

Per Serving
Calories: 185; Fat: 14g; Sat. Fat: 7g; Carbs: 2.6g; Protein: 13g

---

Quesadillas
Preparation Time: 5 minutes

Cooking Time: 5 minutes
Total Time: 10 minutes

- 1 medium tomato, sliced
- ½ cup basil, fresh
- 2 whole-wheat tortillas
- ½ teaspoon ground black pepper
- 1 tablespoon olive oil
- 4 large eggs, scrambled
- ½ cup grated mozzarella cheese, low-fat

1. Take a medium bowl, place scrambled eggs in it, add black pepper, and stir until combined.
2. Take a large plate, place the tortillas, and spread the scrambled eggs on half of each tortilla.
3. Add basil, tomatoes, and mozzarella on top of the eggs, and then fold the tortillas, covering the filling.
4. Take a medium pan, place it over medium heat, add oil and when hot, place the tortillas and cook for 3 to 4 minutes per side until golden.
5. When done, place the prepared tortillas on a serving plate, cut them into slices and serve.

Per Serving
Calories: 201; Fat: 10g; Sat. Fat: 4g; Carbs: 15g; Protein: 12.5g

Italian Fried Calamari

Preparation Time: 20 minutes
Cooking Time: 5 minutes
Total Time: 25 minutes

- 1 lb. squid rings (about 450 grams) (cut the squid into circles)
- A neutral-flavored oil with a high smoke point for frying (such as peanut oil or refined coconut oil)
- 4 medium eggs
- 2/3 cup unbleached flour for all purposes
- 4 tablespoons semolina
- 1 lemon (cut into pieces)
- Salt

1. Rinse squid pieces in running water and dry thoroughly with paper towels.
2. Heat a few inches of the oil in a large, high-walled pan with a thick bottom over medium heat or 350°F.
3. Place the flour in a shallow bowl. Beat the eggs in a large bowl.
4. Place the semolina in a small bowl. Dip the squid rings in the flour and shake them to remove the excess. Dip in the egg and then in the semolina before frying them in the hot oil.
5. Fry calamari in different batches to avoid overcrowding until you get a crisp, light brown texture, about one to two minutes.
6. Transfer the fried squid to a dish with absorbent paper to drain. Season with salt and serve with lemon slices.

Per Serving:
Calories: 333; Fat: 11g; Carbs: 29g; Protein: 29g

Roasted Chickpeas

Preparation Time: 5 minutes
Cooking Time: 15 minutes
Total Time: 20 minutes

- 2 cups cooked chickpeas
- 1/3 teaspoon salt
- ¼ teaspoon dried oregano
- ¼ teaspoon garlic powder
- ¼ teaspoon ground black pepper
- 1 tablespoon olive oil
- 1 teaspoon red wine vinegar
- 1 teaspoon lemon juice

1. Switch on the oven, set it to 218 degrees C or 425 degrees F, and let it preheat.
2. Take a baking tray, line it with parchment paper, arrange the chickpeas on it in a single layer.
3. Place the baking sheet in the oven. Roast the chickpeas for 10 minutes until tender-crisp and golden brown, tossing halfway through.
4. Take a large bowl, place salt, black pepper, oregano, garlic powder, black pepper, oil, red wine vinegar, and lemon juice. Stir until combined.
5. Add the roasted chickpeas, toss until well mixed, and then layer the chickpeas mixture on the baking tray.

6. Return it into the oven and then continue roasting for 5 minutes or brown.
7. When done, spoon the mixture into the serving bowl, and serve.

Per Serving
Calories: 238; Fat: 7.8g; Sat. Fat: 1g; Carbs: 32g; Protein: 10.6g

---

Feta Spinach And Sweet Red Pepper Muffins

Prep Time: 10 minutes
Cooking Time: 20 minutes
Total Time: 30 minutes

- 1/3 cup baby spinach leaves
- 1 tablespoon red peppers, jarred, patted dry
- 2/3 cups whole-wheat flour
- 1 tablespoon coconut sugar
- ¼ teaspoon salt
- ½ teaspoon paprika
- ½ teaspoon baking powder
- 1 ½ tablespoon olive oil
- 1 medium egg, at room temperature
- 1 tablespoon almond milk, low-fat, unsweetened
- 1 tablespoon crumbled feta cheese, low-fat

1. Switch on the oven, set it to 190 degrees C or 375 degrees F, and preheat.

2. Meanwhile, take six silicone muffin cups, line them with muffin liners, and spray them with cooking spray to grease them.
3. Take a medium bowl, add flour, sugar, salt, paprika, and baking powder and mix until blended.
4. Take a medium bowl, crack an egg in it, pour in the oil and milk, and whisk until mixed.
5. Then add the prepared egg mixture into the flour mixture, ½ cup at a time, stir until combined, and a thick dough forms.
6. Add feta cheese, spinach, and red peppers, stir until incorporated, and divide the mixture evenly among the prepared muffin cups.
7. Place the muffin cups in the oven, and bake for 20 to 25 minutes, or until firm and the top turns golden brown.
8. When done, let muffins cool at room temperature for 5 minutes and then serve.

Per Serving
Calories: 290; Fat: 14g; Sat. Fat: 2g; Carbs: 34g; Protein: 12g

---

Baked Beet Chips

Preparation Time: 5 minutes
Cooking Time: 10 minutes
Total Time: 15 minutes

- 2 large beets, trimmed, scrubbed, sliced
- ½ tablespoon dried chives
- ½ tablespoon salt

- 1 tablespoon olive oil

1. Switch on the oven, set it to 204 degrees C or 400 degrees F, and let it preheat.
2. Meanwhile, take a baking tray, drizzle oil, spread it all around to grease the tray, and then set it aside until required.
3. Place the beets on the prepared baking tray in a single layer and then bake for 10 minutes, until crispy.
4. Take a small bowl, place salt and chives, and stir until mixed.
5. When the beet chips have baked, sprinkle the prepared salt mixture on top, and let the beets cool at room temperature.
6. Toss the beet chips and then serve.

Per Serving
Calories: 110.4; Fat: 2.4g; Sat. Fat: 0.6g; Carbs: 14g; Protein: 2.6g

---

Roasted Pumpkin Seeds
Preparation Time: 5 minutes
Cooking Time: 15 minutes
Total Time: 20 minutes

- 1 cup pumpkin seeds, rinsed, dried
- ¼ teaspoon salt
- ¼ teaspoon ground black pepper
- 1 teaspoon olive oil

1. Switch on the oven, set it to 204 degrees C or 400 degrees F, and let it preheat.

2. Meanwhile, take a large bowl, place pumpkin seeds in it, drizzle with oil, toss until well coated, then stir in salt and black pepper until well mixed.
3. Take a baking sheet, line it with a sheet of parchment, sprinkle the pumpkin seeds on top in a single layer, and then bake for 12-15 minutes until crispy.
4. When done, let the pumpkin seeds rest for 5 minutes and then serve.

Per Serving
Calories: 169; Fat: 14g; Sat. Fat: 2.5g; Carbs: 4.3g; Protein: 8.8g

---

Beet Hummus
Preparation Time: 5 minutes
Cooking Time: 0 minutes
Total Time: 5 minutes

- 1 small beet, cooked, peeled, and chopped
- ¼ teaspoon minced garlic
- ½ cup chickpeas, canned, drained, and rinsed
- ¼ teaspoon salt
- ¼ teaspoon ground black pepper
- 2 tablespoons olive oil
- 1 teaspoon tahini
- 2 teaspoons lemon juice

1. In a food processor, place chickpeas and add oil, beet, lemon juice, tahini and garlic.

2. Pulse for 1 minute or more until well combined, add salt and black pepper and pulse until well-mixed and smooth.
3. When done, spoon the prepared hummus into the serving bowl, and serve with favorite crackers and vegetable slices.

Per Serving
Calories: 112; Fat: 7g; Sat. Fat: 1.3g; Carbs: 10g; Protein: 2.1g

3. Toast the bread in the skillet for 2 to 4 minutes or until golden brown. Flip the bread halfway through the cooking time.
4. Lastly, assemble the bread with the mixture to make the sandwich and serve warm.

Per Serving
Calories: 270; Fat: 15g; Sat. Fat: 3g; Carbs: 26g; Protein: 17g

Tuna Salad Sandwiches
Preparation Time: 10 minutes
Cooking Time: 5 minutes
Total Time: 15 minutes

- 6 oz white tuna, drained
- 1 roasted red pepper, diced
- Juice of 1 lemon
- ½ small red onion, diced
- 10 olives, pitted and finely chopped
- ¼ cup plain Greek yogurt
- 1 tbsp parsley, chopped
- Salt and freshly ground pepper, to taste
- 1 tbsp olive oil
- 4 pieces whole-grain bread

1. Combine all ingredients, except the bread and olive oil, in a medium bowl, then stir to mix well.
2. Heat the olive oil in a non-stick skillet over medium-high heat.

Kale Chips
Preparation Time: 10 minutes
Cooking Time: 20 minutes
Total Time: 30 minutes

- 2 large bunches of kale, ribs removed (rinsed & patted dry)
- 1 tbsp extra-virgin olive oil
- 1 tsp salt

1. Preheat the oven to 250°F.
2. Grease 2 baking sheets.
3. Next, tear the kales into large pieces and toss them with olive oil. Arrange on baking sheets.
4. Sprinkle with salt.
5. Bake for 20 minutes until dry and crisp
6. Serve warm.

Per Serving
Calories: 38; Fat: 3g; Sat. Fat: 1g; Carbs: 3g; Protein: 2g

Peach Caprese Skewers

Preparation Time: 5 minutes
Cooking Time: 0 minutes
Total Time: 5 minutes

- 2 medium peaches slices
- 1 cup cherry tomatoes
- ½ cup baby mozzarella balls
- 6 fresh basil leaves

1. Thread peach slices, tomatoes, mozzarella balls, and basil alternately onto skewers.

Per Serving
Calories: 143; Fat: 5,6g; Sat. Fat: 3g; Carbs: 17.3g; Protein: 7,2g

Hummus

Preparation Time: 5 minutes
Cooking Time: 0 minutes
Total Time: 5 minutes

- 1 cup cooked chickpeas
- ½ teaspoon minced garlic

- ½ teaspoon salt
- ½ teaspoon lemon pepper seasoning
- 2 teaspoons olive oil
- 2 tablespoons tahini paste
- 2 teaspoons lemon juice
- 2 cubes of ice

1. Place in a food processor, add the chickpeas and garlic and pulse for 30 seconds or more until smooth and powder-like in consistency.
2. Then add tahini, salt, ice cube, and lemon juice, and pulse until the mixture is well combined and smooth.
3. When done, spoon the hummus into a bowl, drizzle oil on it, sprinkle with the lemon pepper seasoning and serve with favorite crackers and vegetable slices.

Per Serving
Calories: 176; Fat: 8.7g; Sat. Fat: 1.2g; Carbs: 19.4 g; Protein: 7.2g

Eggplant Dip

Preparation Time: 10 minutes
Cooking Time: 10 minutes
Total Time: 20 minutes

- 1 small eggplant
- 1 small tomato, diced
- 4 tablespoons diced cucumber
- ½ cup parsley leaves
- ½ teaspoon chopped garlic
- ¼ teaspoon salt, divided

- ¼ teaspoon ground black pepper, divided
- ½ teaspoon lemon pepper seasoning
- ¼ teaspoon Aleppo pepper
- 1 tablespoon tahini paste
- 1 tablespoon olive oil
- ¾ tablespoon yogurt, low-fat, unsweetened
- ½ tablespoon lemon juice, divided

1 Turn the stove on medium heat, place the eggplant on the burner, and then cook for 8 to 10 minutes until charred, rotate occasionally.
2 When done, transfer the eggplant to a plate, let it cool, and then peel it.
3 Place the peeled eggplant on a drainer, let it rest for 3 minutes to drain any liquid, and then place in a food processor.
4 Add garlic, tahini, yogurt, lemon juice, salt, black pepper, lemon pepper seasoning, and Aleppo pepper, and then pulse for 1 minute until smooth.
5 Spoon the prepared dip into a serving bowl, cover the bowl with its lid, place in a refrigerator and let it rest for 30 minutes.
6 Meanwhile, take a medium bowl, add tomato, cucumber, parsley, salt, and black pepper, drizzle with oil and lemon juice, and stir until well mixed.
7 After 30 minutes, let the eggplant dip rest at room temperature for 10 minutes, top with the prepared tomato mixture, and then serve with crackers.

Per Serving
Calories: 138; Fat: 9.4g; Sat. Fat: 2g; Carbs: 13.8g; Protein: 2.4g

SOUP AND SALADS

Cucumber and Tomato Salad

Preparation Time: 10 minutes
Cooking Time: 0 minutes
Total Time: 10 minutes

- Salt and black pepper, to taste
- 1 tablespoon fresh lemon juice
- 1/2 onion, chopped
- 1/2 cucumber, peeled and diced
- 1 tomato, chopped
- 2 cups spinach

1. In a salad bowl, mix the onion, cucumbers, and tomatoes. Season with pepper and salt to taste.
2. Add the lemon juice and mix well. Add the spinach, toss to coat, serve and enjoy.

Serving Suggestion: Top with feta cheese and chickpeas.

Per Serving:
Calories 70.3; Fat 0.3g; Carbs 8.9g; Protein 2.2g

Pear Salad with Roquefort Cheese

Preparation Time: 20 minutes
Cooking Time: 10 minutes
Total Time: 30 minutes

- 1 leaf lettuce, torn into bite-sized pieces
- 3 pears - peeled, cored and diced
- 5 ounces Roquefort, crumbled
- 1 avocado - peeled, seeded and diced
- 1/2 cup chopped green onions
- 1/4 cup white sugar
- 1/2 cup pecan nuts
- 1/3 cup olive oil
- 3 tablespoons red wine vinegar
- 1 1/2 teaspoon of white sugar
- 1 1/2 teaspoon of prepared mustard
- 1/2 teaspoon of salted black pepper
- 1 clove of garlic

1. Mix 1/4 cup of sugar with the pecans in a large skillet over medium-low heat. Continue to stir gently until the sugar has melted and is caramelized with pecans. Carefully transfer the nuts to wax paper. Allow to cool and break into pieces.
2. Mix vinaigrette oil, vinegar, 1 1/2 teaspoon of sugar, mustard, chopped garlic, salt, and pepper.
3. Add lettuce, pears, blue cheese, avocado, and green onions in a large bowl. Pour vinaigrette over salad, sprinkle with pecans and serve.

Per Serving:
Calories: 426; Fat: 31.6 g; Carbs: 33.1 g; Protein: 8 g

Broccoli With Caramelized Onions & Pine Nuts

Preparation Time: 10 minutes
Cooking Time: 25 minutes
Total Time: 35 minutes

- 2 tbsp pine nuts with chopped slivered almonds
- 1 tsp olive oil extra-virgin
- 1/2 cup chopped onion
- ¼ tsp salt
- 2 cups of broccoli florets
- 1 tsp balsamic vinegar
- 1 Freshly ground pepper to taste

1. Toast pine nuts (or almonds) over medium-low heat in a medium-dry skillet, constantly stirring for (2 - 3) minutes, until lightly browned and fragrant. To cool, transfer it to a small bowl.
2. In the pan, add oil and heat over medium heat. Add the onion and salt; cook for 15 to 20 minutes, occasionally stirring, adjusting the heat as needed, until soft and golden brown.
3. Meanwhile, steam the broccoli for 4 to 6 minutes, until just tender. Transfer to a big bowl. Add the nuts, onion, pepper and vinegar; toss to coat. Immediately serve.

Per Serving:
Calories: 102; Protein: 3.4g; Carbs: 9g; Fat: 6.9g

- 1 large eggplant
- 1 diced plum tomato
- 1 ½ tsp red wine vinegar
- ½ tsp kosher salt to taste
- ½ tsp chopped fresh oregano
- 1 finely chopped garlic cloves
- 3 tbsp extra virgin olive oil
- 3 tbsp chopped parsley
- Black pepper to taste
- Capers

1. Heat the grill medium-high. Prick eggplant with a fork all over, place on the grill and close the lid; cook for 15 minutes, occasionally turning, until eggplant is very soft and the skin is blistered.
2. Pull out the insides of the eggplants when they are fairly fresh and coarsely chop them. Transfer the tomatoes, vinegar, salt, oregano and garlic to a bowl and toss. Stir in the parsley and oil; season with more salt and pepper if necessary. If you like them, garnish them with capers. Use warm pita bread to serve.

Per Serving:
Calories: 252; Fat: 16.4g; Carbs: 18.8g; Protein: 6.3g

Grilled Eggplant Salad
Preparation Time: 10 minutes
Cooking Time: 15 minutes
Total Time: 25 minutes

Mushroom Seared Salad With Blue Cheese And Arugula
Preparation Time: 10 minutes
Cooking Time: 10 minutes
Total Time: 20 minutes

- 1-pound portobello sliced mushrooms
- ¼ cup of extra virgin olive oil
- ¼ cup of red wine
- ¼ tsp salt
- ¼ tsp pepper
- 1 tsp thyme
- 2 cups of arugula
- 2 medium tomatoes cut into wedges
- 1/4 of a sliced thinly red onion
- ¼ cup of blue cheese
- 1/2 cup of croutons
- ⅓ cup of balsamic vinegar

1. Heat olive oil in a medium-hot skillet. Stir in the mushrooms and sauté for about 1 minute. Add the red wine, salt, thyme, and pepper. Sauté, frequently stirring, until mushrooms have absorbed liquid (about 10 minutes). Remove it from the heat.
2. Add the arugula and the tomatoes to a large salad bowl. Arugula is covered with warm mushrooms. Combine the red onion salad, blue cheese, croutons, and balsamic vinegar. Instantly serve.

Per Serving:
Calories 222; Fat 0.6 g; Carbs 58.2 g; Protein 1.3 g

Pasta And Chickpea Soup
Preparation Time: 5 minutes
Cooking Time: 15 minutes
Total Time: 20 minutes

- 15 ounces cherry tomatoes, canned, drained
- ½ teaspoon crushed dried rosemary
- 1 teaspoon chopped garlic
- 12 ounces cooked chickpeas, divided
- 3 ounces whole-wheat pasta
- ¼ teaspoon ground black pepper
- 1 teaspoon olive oil
- 3 tablespoons grated parmesan cheese, low-fat
- 15 ounces beef broth, sodium-reduced
- 1 cup water

1. Take a medium pot, place it over low heat, add oil and when hot, add garlic and cook for a minute until fragrant and golden.
2. Then add tomatoes, and rosemary, simmer for 3 minutes and then take a potato masher to crush the tomatoes.
3. Pour in the beef broth and water, turn on medium-high heat and bring the soup to a boil.
4. Take a medium bowl, place half of the chickpeas, and with a potato masher, crush the chickpeas.
5. Add the crushed chickpeas into the soup along with the pasta and black pepper and stir until combined.
6. Let the soup simmer for 7 minutes or until the pasta has cooked, then add the remaining chickpeas into the soup, and stir until well mixed.
7. When done, spoon the prepared soup into a serving bowl, and serve.

Per Serving
Calories: 307; Fat: 4.8g; Sat. Fat: 1.6g; Carbs: 53.6g; Protein: 13.6g

Lentil Soup

Preparation Time: 5 minutes
Cooking Time: 30 minutes
Total Time: 35 minutes

- 2 tablespoons minced onion
- ½ of a large carrot, chopped
- 1 teaspoon minced garlic
- 4-ounce brown lentils
- ¼ teaspoon dried rosemary
- ¼ teaspoon dried oregano
- 1 bay leaf
- ¼ teaspoon salt
- ¼ teaspoon ground black pepper
- 2 tablespoons olive oil, divided
- 1 teaspoon tomato paste
- 2 tablespoons water and more as needed

1 Take a medium pot, place it over medium heat, add the lentils, pour enough water to cover the lentils by 1 inch over the lentils, and cook for 10 minutes.
2 When lentils are cooked, drain, transfer to a medium bowl, and set aside until required.
3 Take a medium saucepan, place it over medium heat, add oil, and when hot, add garlic, onion, and carrot, and cook for 3 to 4 minutes until softened.
4 Then add lentils, oregano, rosemary, and bay leaf, pour in the water, and then bring the soup to a boil.

5 Then switch heat to medium-low level, cover the pot with its lid, and continue simmering the soup for 5 minutes.
6 Then add tomato paste, salt, and black pepper, stir until mixed, cover the pot with its lid, and let it cook for15 minutes, or until lentils have turned soft.
7 When done, divide the soup evenly between two bowls, drizzle oil on top, and serve.

Per Serving
Calories: 285; Fat: 12.4g; Sat. Fat: 1.7g; Carbs: 32.2g; Protein: 12.4g

Creamy White Bean Soup

Preparation Time: 5 minutes
Cooking Time: 20 minutes
Total Time: 25 minutes

- ¾ cup spinach, sliced
- ½ of a medium white onion, peeled, chopped
- ½ of a medium stalk celery, chopped
- ½ of a medium carrot, chopped
- ½ teaspoon minced garlic
- 12-ounce cooked white kidney beans
- ¼ teaspoon ground black pepper
- ¼ teaspoon dried thyme
- 1 teaspoon olive oil
- 7 ounces chicken broth
- 1 teaspoon lemon juice
- 1 cup water

1. Take a medium saucepan, place it over medium heat, add oil and when hot, add celery, carrot, and onion, and cook for 5 minutes or until softened.
2. Add garlic, cook for a minute until golden, add beans, black pepper, thyme, pour in the broth and water, stir until mixed, and then bring it to a boil.
3. Cook the soup for 10 minutes, remove half of the beans and vegetables from the prepared soup and set it aside until required.
4. Remove pan from heat and then pulse it with an electric hand mixer until smooth.
5. Return the saucepan over medium heat, bring the soup to a boil, add spinach, and lemon juice, cook for 3 to 4 minutes until spinach leaves have wilted.
6. When done, divide the soup evenly between two bowls, and serve.

Per Serving
Calories: 245; Fat: 4.9g; Sat. Fat: 0.5g; Carbs: 38.1g; Protein: 12g

Mediterranean Salad

Preparation Time: 10 minutes
Cooking Time: 0 minutes
Total Time: 10 minutes

- 1 cup diced tomatoes
- 1 diced cucumber
- ¼ cup chopped parsley, fresh
- ¼ teaspoon salt
- ¼ teaspoon ground black pepper
- ¼ teaspoon ground sumac
- 1 ½ teaspoon olive oil
- 1 teaspoon lemon juice

1. Take a medium bowl, add tomato, cucumber, salt, and parsley, toss until well mixed, and then set aside for 5 minutes.
2. Then add sumac and oil, and then toss until combined.
3. Divide the salad between two bowls and then serve.

Per Serving
Calories: 62; Fat: 4.9g; Sat. Fat: 0.7g; Carbs: 4.8g; Protein: 1g

Veggie & Chicken Soup

Preparation Time: 15 minutes
Cooking Time: 20 minutes
Total Time: 35 minutes

- 1/2 cup mushrooms, chopped
- 1 tsp olive oil
- 1 large carrot, chopped
- 1/2 yellow onion, chopped
- 1/2 celery stalk, chopped
- 1 yellow squash, chopped
- 1 chicken breast, cubed
- ½ cup chopped fresh parsley
- 2 cups chicken stock
- Salt and black pepper to taste

1. Warm the oil in a skillet over lower-medium heat. Place in carrot, onion, mushrooms, and celery and cook for 5 minutes.
2. Stir in chicken and cook for 12 more mins. Mix in squash, salt, and black pepper.
3. Cook for 5 minutes, lower the heat and pour in the stock.
4. Cook covered for 10 more minutes. Divide between bowls and scatter with parsley.
5. Serve immediately.

Per Serving:
Calories: 335; Fat: 9g; Carbs: 28g; Protein: 33g

1. Warm the olive oil in a medium skillet over medium heat and cook onion, celery, mushrooms, carrots, and thyme for 5 minutes until tender. Stir in vegetable stock and lamb and bring to a boil. Lower the heat and simmer for 20 minutes.
2. Mix in chickpeas and cook for another 5 minutes. Ladle your soup into individual bowls.
3. Top with cilantro and serve hot.

Per Serving:
Calories: 300; Fat: 12g; Carbs: 23g; Protein: 15g

Leftover Lamb & Mushroom Soup

Preparation Time: 5 minutes
Cooking Time: 25 minutes
Total Time: 30 minutes

- 1 carrot, chopped
- 1/2 red onion, chopped
- 1 tbsp olive oil
- 1 celery stalks, chopped
- 1 garlic clove, minced
- Salt and black pepper to taste
- 1/2 tbsp thyme, chopped
- 2 cups vegetable stock
- 1/2 cup white mushrooms, sliced
- 4 oz leftover lamb, shredded
- 7 oz canned chickpeas, drained
- 1 tbsp cilantro, chopped

Roasted Cauliflower Soup

Preparation Time: 15 minutes
Cooking Time: 20 minutes
Total Time: 30 minutes

- 1 ½ cup cauliflower florets
- ½ of a small white onion, peeled, chopped
- 1 teaspoon chopped garlic
- ¼ teaspoon salt, divided
- ¼ teaspoon ground black pepper
- 2 teaspoons olive oil
- 2 cups water, divided

1. Switch on the oven's broiler, place the oven rack on the high shelf, and let it preheat.
2. Take a baking tray, line it with aluminum foil, and set it aside until required.
3. Take a large bowl, place cauliflower florets, drizzle with water, and stir in salt.

4   Let the florets rest for 10 minutes, then drain the water out, scatter the florets on the prepared baking tray, and spray evenly with cooking spray.

5   Place the baking tray in the oven and broil the florets for 15 to 30 minutes or until golden brown on top.

6   Then take a large saucepan, place it over medium heat, add oil, and when hot, add onion and cook for 3 minutes until softened.

7   Add garlic, salt, black pepper, water, and roasted florets into the saucepan, and simmer for 15 to 20 minutes or until florets turn soft.

8   Then remove the pan from the heat, use an electric hand mixer to blend the soup until smooth and creamy, and then serve.

Per Serving
Calories: 186; Fat: 12.2g; Sat. Fat: 1.7g; Carbs: 17.6g; Protein: 5.6 g

Tomato Stuffed With Cheese & Peppers

Preparation Time: 10 minutes
Cooking Time: 25 minutes
Total Time: 35 minutes

- 4 tomatoes
- ½ lb. mixed bell peppers, chopped
- 1 tbsp olive oil
- 2 garlic cloves, minced
- ½ cup diced onion
- 1 tbsp chopped oregano
- 1 tbsp chopped basil
- 1 cup shredded mozzarella cheese
- 1 tbsp grated Parmesan cheese
- Salt and black pepper to taste

1 Preheat oven to 370 F. Cut the tops of the tomatoes and scoop out the pulp. Chop the pulp and set it aside. Arrange the tomatoes on a baking sheet lined with baking paper. Warm the olive oil in a pan over medium heat. Add in garlic, onion, basil, bell peppers, oregano, and cook for 5 minutes.
2 Sprinkle with salt and pepper. Remove from the heat and mix in tomato pulp and mozzarella cheese. Divide the mixture between the tomatoes and top with Parmesan cheese.
3 Bake for 20 min. or until the cheese melts. Serve hot.

Per Serving
Calories: 285, Fat: 10g, Carbs: 28g, Protein: 24g

Spiralized Carrot With Peas

Preparation Time: 10 minutes
Cooking Time: 10 minutes
Total Time: 20 minutes

- 2 carrots, spiralized into noodles
- 1/2 sweet onion, chopped
- 1 cup peas
- 1 garlic clove, minced
- 1 tbsp olive oil
- ¼ cup chopped fresh parsley
- Salt and black pepper to taste

1 Heat 1 tbsp of olive oil in a pot over medium heat and sauté the onion and garlic for 3 minutes until just tender and fragrant. Add in spiralized carrots and cook for 4 minutes. Mix in peas, salt, and pepper and cook for 4 minutes.
2 Drizzle with the remaining olive oil and sprinkle with parsley to serve.

Per Serving:
Calories: 157, Fat: 7.3g, Carbs: 19.6g, Protein: 4.8g

Eggplant, Arugula & Sweet Potato Mix

Preparation Time: 10 minutes
Cooking Time: 15 minutes
Total Time: 25 minutes

- 2 cups arugula
- 1 baby eggplant, cubed
- 1 sweet potato, cubed
- 1 tbsp olive oil
- 1/2 red onion, cut into wedges
- 1 tsp hot paprika
- 1 tsp cumin, ground
- Salt and black pepper to taste
- ¼ cup lime juice

1. Warm the olive oil in a medium skillet over medium heat and cook eggplant and potatoes for 5 minutes.
2. Stir in onion, paprika, cumin, salt, pepper, and lime juice and cook for another 10 minutes.
3. Mix in arugula and serve.

Per Serving:
Calories: 210, Fat: 9g, Carbs: 13g, Protein: 5g

Catalan-Style Spinach
Preparation Time: 10 minutes
Cooking Time: 5 minutes
Total Time: 15 minutes

- 2 cups fresh baby spinach
- 1/2 garlic clove, minced
- 1 tbsp raisins, soaked
- 1 tbsp toasted pine nuts
- 1 tbsp olive oil
- Salt and black pepper to taste

1 Warm olive oil in a large skillet over moderate heat and sauté spinach and garlic

for 3 minutes until spinach wilts. Mix in raisins, pine nuts, salt, and pepper and cook for 3 minutes. Serve immediately.

Per Serving:
Calories: 111, Fat: 10g, Carbs: 5.5g, Protein: 1.8g

Simple Sautéed Cauliflower
Preparation Time: 10 minutes
Cooking Time: 15 minutes
Total Time: 25 minutes

- 1/2 onion, chopped
- 1/2 head cauliflower
- ¼ cup olive oil
- 1/2 cup cherry tomatoes
- 2 tablespoons raisins
- 1/2 teaspoon white sugar
- 1/2 garlic clove, minced
- 1/2 teaspoon dried parsley
- ¼ teaspoon red pepper flakes
- 1 tablespoon lemon juice

1. Heat some olive oil in a 10-inch skillet on medium heat. Mix in the onion and cook until soft (about 5–10 minutes are enough).
2. Add the cauliflower, cherry tomatoes, raisins, and white sugar to the onion. Cover the skillet and cook, stirring regularly, until the cauliflower is soft, for about 4–5 minutes.
3. Mix the garlic, parsley, and some red pepper flakes in the cauliflower mixture. Turn the heat up to maximum.
4. Sauté for 1–3 minutes until the cauliflower is browned.

5. Drizzle the juice of the lemon over the cauliflower.

Variation Tip: You can also use fresh parsley.

Per Serving:
Calories: 196.5; Fat: 13.9g; Carbs: 17.8g; Protein: 3.7g

Feta And Cheese Couscous

Preparation Time: 10 minutes
Cooking Time: 15 minutes
Total Time: 25 minutes

- 2 cups sliced green lettuce
- ¼ cup shredded cucumber
- 5-ounce chopped spinach, fresh or thawed if frozen
- 2 tablespoons minced red onion
- 2 tablespoons snipped dill, fresh
- ¼ cup whole-wheat couscous
- ¼ teaspoon salt
- ¼ teaspoon ground black pepper
- ⅛ teaspoon garlic powder, divided
- 1 tablespoon olive oil, divided
- ¼ cup yogurt, low-fat
- ¼ cup silken tofu, mashed
- ¼ cup crumbled feta cheese
- ½ cup water

1 Take a small pot, place it over medium heat, pour in water, and then add couscous.
2 Cover the pot with its lid, remove it from heat, let the couscous stand for 5 minutes and then fluff it with a fork.
3 Make the yogurt sauce, take a small bowl and put the yogurt in it. Add the

cucumber, garlic powder and salt, and stir until blended, and set aside until required.

4 Take a medium bowl, place tofu in it, add spinach, onion, feta cheese, black pepper, garlic powder, dill, and couscous, stir until well combined, and then shape the mixture evenly into four patties.
5 Take a large skillet, place it over medium heat, add oil, and when hot, add the prepared patties and cook for 3 to 4 minutes per side until golden brown.
6 Then place the prepared patties onto a serving plate, add lettuce on the sides, drizzle the prepared yogurt dip on top, and serve.

Per Serving
Calories: 317; Fat: 14.3g; Sat. Fat: 4.9g; Carbs: 34.5g; Protein: 16.2g

Vegetable Cakes

Preparation Time: 10 minutes
Cooking Time: 18 minutes
Total Time: 28 minutes

- ½ cup chopped white onion
- 1 cup chopped spinach, fresh
- 1 small parsnip, grated
- ¼ cup artichoke hearts
- ¼ cup chopped kalamata olives
- 1 teaspoon chopped garlic
- 2 tablespoons chopped sun-dried tomatoes
- 1 ½ teaspoon chopped walnuts
- ¼ cup whole-wheat flour
- ¼ teaspoon salt

- ¼ teaspoon ground black pepper
- 2 tablespoons olive oil, divided
- 1 small egg, beaten

1. Take a medium skillet, place it over medium heat, add oil and when hot, add onion and garlic and cook for 3 minutes until softened.
2. Add spinach, cook for 5 minutes until wilted, transfer the mixture into a large bowl, and set it aside to cool at room temperature.
3. When cooled, add flour, egg, parsnip, artichoke, olives, tomato, salt, and black pepper, stir until well combined, and then shape the mixture into evenly sized patties.
4. Take a medium skillet, place it over medium heat, add oil, and when hot, place the prepared patties and cook for 4 to 5 minutes per side until golden brown.
5. When done, place it on a serving plate, and serve.

Per Serving
Calories: 223; Fat: 15.8g; Sat. Fat: 2.4g; Carbs: 15.4g; Protein: 7.1 g

Grilled Eggplant With Basil And Parsley
Preparation Time: 5 minutes
Cooking Time: 10 minutes
Total Time: 15 minutes

- ½ of a large eggplant, sliced into rounds
- 1 tablespoon chopped basil, fresh

- ½ tablespoon chopped parsley, fresh
- 1 teaspoon minced garlic
- ¼ teaspoon salt
- 3 tablespoons olive oil, divided

1. Take a griddle pan, grease it with 1 tablespoon oil, place it over medium-high heat and let it preheat.
2. Take a large plate, place the eggplant rounds and brush with 1 tablespoon oil until coated.
3. Prepare the garlic mixture. Take a small bowl, add garlic, salt, and the remaining oil, stir until mixed, and then set it aside until required.
4. Place the prepared eggplant on the grill, and then cook for 4 minutes per side until golden brown.
5. When done, transfer the eggplant slices on a serving plate, sprinkle basil and parsley on top, drizzle with the prepared garlic mixture, and serve.

Per Serving
Calories: 203; Fat: 19g; Sat. Fat: 2.7g; Carbs: 8.4g; Protein: 1.5g

Mediterranean Roasted Broccoli & Tomatoes
Preparation Time: 20 minutes
Cooking Time: 10 minutes
Total Time: 30 minutes

- ¼ teaspoon salt
- ½ teaspoon freshly grated lemon zest
- 1 tablespoon lemon juice
- 5 black olives (pitted, sliced)
- 1/2 teaspoon dried oregano
- 1 teaspoon capers, rinsed (optional)
- 6 ounces broccoli preferably cut into florets (about 4 cups)
- 1/2 cup grape tomatoes
- 1 tablespoon extra-virgin olive oil
- 1 garlic clove (minced)

1. Preheat the oven to 450°F.
2. Throw broccoli, tomatoes, oil, garlic, and salt in a large bowl until evenly coated.
3. Spread in a uniform layer on a baking sheet. Bake until the broccoli begins to brown (10 to 13 minutes).
4. Meanwhile, combine lemon zest and juice, olives, oregano, and capers (optional) in a large bowl.
5. Add the evenly roasted vegetables and stir to combine.
6. Serve warm or let it cool down before refrigerating.

Per Serving
Calories: 68; Fat: 4g; Carbs: 7,8; Protein: 3g

Orzo With Herbs
Preparation Time: 20 minutes
Cooking Time: 10 minutes
Total Time: 30 minutes

- 1 cup orzo
- ½ cup fresh basil, finely chopped
- ½ cup fresh parsley, finely chopped

- 1 tbsp lemon zest

Dressing
- ½ cup extra-virgin olive oil
- ⅓ cup lemon juice
- 1 tsp salt
- ½ tsp freshly ground black pepper

1. Put the orzo in a large saucepan with boiling water and allow it to cook for 6 minutes.
2. Drain the orzo in a sieve and rinse well under cold running water. Set aside to cool completely.
3. When cooled, place the orzo in a large bowl. Mix in the basil, lemon zest, and parsley. Set it aside.
4. Make the dressing: In a separate bowl, combine the olive oil, lemon juice, salt, and pepper, then stir to incorporate.
5. 5. Pour the dressing into the bowl of orzo mixture and toss gently until everything is well combined.
6. Serve immediately, or refrigerate for later.

Per Serving
Calories: 160; Fat: 4,6g; Sat Fat: 0.7g; Carbs: 30.4g; Protein: 3g

Basil Artichoke
Preparation Time: 10 minutes
Cooking Time: 10 minutes
Total Time: 20 minutes

- ½ teaspoon minced garlic
- ½ teaspoon salt
- ½ teaspoon chili flakes

- ¼ cup apple cider vinegar
- 1 cup artichoke hearts, frozen
- 1 tablespoon olive oil
- 2 teaspoons fresh basil, chopped

1. Heat a pan with oil over medium-high heat, add garlic and apple cider vinegar. Cook the liquid for 1minute.
2. Add all remaining ingredients and stir well.
3. Cook the meal for 9 minutes with the closed lid.

Per Serving

Calories: 40; Fat: 3.4; Carbs: 1.8g; Protein: 0.5g

Chili Broccoli

Preparation Time: 10 minutes
Cooking Time: 10 minutes
Total Time: 20 minutes

- 1 cup broccoli, roughly chopped
- 1 teaspoon chili powder
- 1 tablespoon avocado oil
- 1 bell pepper, diced

1. Heat the avocado oil in the skillet.
2. Add broccoli and roast it for 5 minutes.
3. Then sprinkle the vegetables with chili powder and bell pepper.
4. Stir the ingredients carefully and close the lid.
5. Cook the meal for 5 minutes more.

Per Serving

Calories: 58; Fat: 4.3g; Carbs: 5.2g; Protein: 1.4g

Cauliflower Rica

Preparation Time: 5 minutes
Cooking Time: 10 minutes
Total Time: 15 minutes

- 1 cup cauliflower, shredded
- 1 tablespoon olive oil
- 1 oz Parmesan, grated
- 1 cup chicken stock

1. Bring the chicken stock to boil and add shredded cauliflower.
2. Boil it for 5 minutes.
3. Then drain the liquid and mix cauliflower with oil and Parmesan.
4. Stir the meal carefully.

Per Serving:

Calories: 63; Fat: 4.6g; Carbs: 3.5g; Protein: 3.5g

Vegetable Rice Bowl

Preparation Time: 15 minutes
Cooking Time: 15 minutes
Total Time: 30 minutes

- 6 oz broccoli cuts
- 2 cups fresh baby spinach
- 1 red chili, seeded and chopped
- 1 cup cooked brown rice
- 2 tbsp olive oil

- 1/2 onion, chopped
- 1 garlic clove, minced
- 1 orange, juiced and zested
- 1 cup vegetable broth
- Salt and black pepper to taste

1. Heat the oil in a skillet over medium-low heat, sauté the onion for 5 minutes, add the broccoli cuts, and cook for 4-5 minutes until tender. Sauté the garlic and red pepper for 30 seconds.
2. Pour in orange zest, orange juice, broth, salt, pepper and bring to a boil.
3. Stir in the rice and spinach and cook for 4 minutes until the liquid is reduced. Serve.

Per Serving:
Calories: 391; Fat: 9.4g; Carbs: 67.6g; Protein: 9.8g

and garlic and stir-fry for 4-5 minutes until tender. Mix in salt, black pepper, 2 tbsp of parsley, five-spice powder, tomato paste, and tomatoes; stir well and cook for 10-12 minutes.

2. Boiling in a pot with salted water, add the pasta and cook until al dente, occasionally stirring for about 8-10 minutes. Drain and stir in the vegetable mixture.
3. Serve topped with Parmesan cheese and remaining fresh parsley.

Per Serving:
Calories: 566; Fat: 21.6g; Carbs: 71.9g; Protein: 24.4g

Parmesan Spaghetti In Mushroom-Tomato Sauce

Preparation Time: 10 minutes
Cooking Time: 20 minutes
Total Time: 30 minutes

- 8 oz spaghetti, cut in half
- 1 cup mushrooms, chopped
- 1/2 bell pepper, chopped
- ½ cup yellow onion, chopped
- 2 garlic cloves, minced
- ½ tsp five-spice powder
- 2 tbsp fresh parsley, chopped
- 1 tbsp tomato paste
- 1 ripe tomato, chopped
- ½ cup Parmesan cheese, grated
- ¼ cup olive oil
- Salt and black pepper to taste

1. Heat 1 cup oil in a skillet over medium-high heat. Add in mushrooms, bell pepper, onion,

FISH AND SEAFOOD

Pesto Fish Fillet

Preparation Time: 10 minutes
Cooking Time: 8 minutes
Total Time: 18 minutes

- 2 halibut fillets
- 1/2 cup water
- 1 tbsp lemon zest, grated
- 1/2 tbsp capers
- 1/2 cup basil, chopped
- 1/2 tbsp garlic, chopped
- 1/2 avocado, peeled and chopped
- Salt and black pepper to taste

1 Add lemon zest, capers, basil, garlic, avocado, pepper, and salt into the blender and blend until smooth.
2 Place fish fillets on aluminum foil and spread the blended mixture on fish fillets. Fold foil around the fish fillets. Pour the water into the pot and place the trivet in the pot. Place the fish foil on the trivet.
3 Cover the pan with a lid and cook over high heat for 8 minutes. Once done, remove the lid. Serve and enjoy.

Per Serving:
Calories: 426; Fat: 16.6 g; Carbs: 5.5 g; Protein: 61.8 g

Salmon And Mango Mix

Preparation Time: 10 minutes
Cooking Time: 25 minutes
Total Time: 35 minutes

- 2 salmon fillets, skinless and boneless
- Salt and pepper to the taste
- 2 tablespoons olive oil
- 2 garlic cloves, minced
- 2 mangos, peeled and cubed
- 1 red chili, chopped
- 1 small piece ginger, grated
- Juice of 1 lime
- 1 tablespoon cilantro, chopped

1 In a roasting pan, combine the salmon with the oil, garlic and the rest of the ingredients except the cilantro; toss, introduce in the oven at 350 degrees F and bake for 25 minutes.
2 Divide everything between plates and serve with the cilantro sprinkled on top.

Per Serving:
Calories: 251; fat: 15.9; carbs: 26.4; protein: 12.4

Trout And Tzatziki Sauce
Preparation Time: 10 minutes
Cooking Time: 10 minutes
Total Time: 20 minutes

- Juice of ½ lime
- Salt and black pepper to the taste
- 1 teaspoon coriander, ground
- 1/2 teaspoon garlic, minced
- 2 trout fillets, boneless
- 1/2 teaspoon sweet paprika
- 1 tablespoon avocado oil

For the sauce:
- 1/2 cucumber, chopped
- 2 garlic cloves, minced
- 1 tablespoon olive oil
- 1 teaspoon white vinegar
- 1 cup Greek yogurt
- A pinch of salt and white pepper

1. Heat a pan with the avocado oil over medium-high heat, add the fish, salt, pepper, lime juice, 1/2 teaspoon garlic and the paprika; rub the fish gently and cook for 4 minutes on each side.
2. In a bowl, combine the cucumber with 4 garlic cloves and the rest of the ingredients for the sauce and whisk well.
3. Divide the fish between plates, drizzle the sauce all over and serve with a side salad.

Per Serving:
Calories: 393; fat: 18.5; carbs: 18.3; protein: 39.6

Healthy Steaks
Preparation Time: 10 minutes
Cooking Time: 20 minutes
Total Time: 30 minutes

- 1 tsp olive oil,
- 8 ounces halibut steak,
- ½ tsp garlic, minced
- 1 tbsp butter,
- Salt and pepper to taste

1. Heat a skillet and add the oil.
2. Over a medium flame, brown the steaks
3. In a pan, melt the butter with garlic, salt and pepper.
4. Add the steaks, toss to coat, and serve.

Per Serving:
Calories: 284, Fat: 17g, Carbs: 1.4g, Protein: 24g

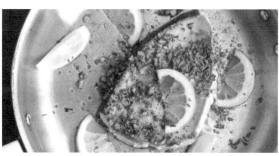

Lemon-Parsley Swordfish
Preparation Time: 10 minutes
Cooking Time: 20 minutes
Total Time: 30 minutes

- 1 cup fresh Italian parsley
- ¼ cup lemon juice
- ¼ cup extra-virgin olive oil
- ¼ cup fresh thyme

- 1 clove garlic
- ½ teaspoon salt
- 2 swordfish steaks
- Olive oil spray

1 Preheat the oven to 450F. Grease a large pan with olive oil spray.
2 Place the parsley, lemon juice, olive oil, thyme, garlic, and salt in a food processor and pulse until smoothly blended.
3 Arrange the swordfish steaks in the greased baking dish and spoon the parsley mixture over the top.
4 Bake for 18 minutes until flaky. Serve the fish among two plates and serve hot.

Per Serving
Calories: 396; fat: 21.7g; protein: 44.2g; carbs: 2.9g

Grilled Octopus
Preparation Time: 10 minutes
Cooking Time: 20 minutes
Total Time: 30 minutes

- ½ teaspoon chopped fresh parsley
- 1-pound octopus, head and beak removed
- ½ teaspoon salt, divided
- ¼ teaspoon ground black pepper
- 1 teaspoon lemon juice
- ½ teaspoon black peppercorns
- 1 teaspoon olive oil
- 1 wine cork

1. Take a large pot half full with water, place it over high heat. Add salt, peppercorns,

and wine cork and bring the mixture to a boil.
2. In the meantime, place the octopus on a cutting board, pound it all over with a wooden spoon.
3. When water begins to boil, add the octopus into it, switch heat to a medium-low temperature, cover the pot with its lid and let it cook for 20 to 30 minutes, or until tender.
4. Then remove the pot from the heat, remove the octopus, and let it cool for 10 minutes at room temperature.
5. Meanwhile, take a griddle pan, grease it with 1 tablespoon oil, place it over medium-high heat and let it preheat.
6. Place the octopus on the griddle pan, cook it for 4 minutes per side until slightly charred, then transfer it to a cutting board and cut it into pieces.
7. Transfer the octopus' pieces to a plate, drizzle with oil and lemon juice, sprinkle with salt, black pepper, and parsley, and then serve.

Per Serving
Calories: 256; Fat: 5.9g; Sat. Fat: 1.06g; Carbs: 7.1g; Protein: 41.2g

Spaghetti With Tuna And Capers
Preparation Time: 5 minutes
Cooking Time: 20 minutes
Total Time: 25 minutes

- 1 small white onion, peeled, sliced
- ½ tablespoon chopped parsley, fresh

- 1 tablespoon capers, drained
- 6 ounces canned tuna, drained
- ½ pound whole-wheat spaghetti
- ¼ teaspoon crushed red flakes
- 1 tablespoon olive oil

1. Take a medium pot half-full water, place it over medium-high heat, bring it to a boil, add spaghetti and cook for 10 minutes until tender.
2. When done, take out ½ cup cooking water, set it aside, and drain the spaghetti.
3. Take a large skillet pan, place it over medium heat, add oil, and when hot, add onion and cook for 5 minutes, or until light brown.
4. Add tuna, capers, and red pepper, stir until mixed and cook for another minute or thoroughly hot.
5. Add the cooked spaghetti, stir until combined, pour in the reserved pasta water, and cook for 2 minutes or thoroughly hot.
6. Sprinkle with parsley and then serve.

Per Serving
Calories: 290; Fat: 9.8g; Sat. Fat: 1.6g; Carbs: 36.8g; Protein: 13.6g

Crusty Halibut
Preparation Time: 20 minutes
Cooking Time: 15 minutes
Total Time: 35 minutes

- Parsley to top
- Fresh dill, 2 tbsp, chopped
- Fresh chives, 2 tbsp, chopped
- Olive oil, 1 tbsp
- Salt and pepper to taste
- Halibut, fillets, 6 ounces
- Lemon zest, ½ tsp, finely grated
- Greek yogurt, 2 tbsp

1. Preheat the oven to 400F.
2. Line a baking sheet with foil.
3. Add all the ingredients to a wide dish, and marinate fillets.
4. Rinse and dry fillets; then add to the oven and bake for 15 minutes.

Per Serving:
Calories: 273, Fat: 7.2g, Carbs: 15g, Protein: 39g

Smokey Glazed Tuna
Preparation Time: 20 minutes
Cooking Time: 10 minutes
Total Time: 30 minutes

- Tuna, 4-ounce steaks
- Orange juice, 1 tbsp
- Minced garlic, ½ clove
- Lemon juice, ½ tsp
- Fresh parsley, 1 tbsp, chopped
- Soy sauce, 1 tbsp
- Extra virgin olive oil, 1 tbsp
- Ground black pepper, ¼ tsp
- Oregano, ¼ tsp

1. Pick a mixing dish, and add all the ingredients, except the tuna.
2. Mix well, and then add the tuna to the marinade.
3. Refrigerate this mixture for 20 minutes.
4. Heat a grill pan and cook the tuna on each side for 5 minutes.
5. Serve when cooked.

Per Serving:
Calories: 200; Fat: 7.9g; Carbs: 3.7g; Protein: 27.4g

Mussels O' Marine
Preparation Time: 20 minutes
Cooking Time: 10 minutes
Total Time: 30 minutes

- Mussels, scrubbed and debearded, 1 pound
- Coconut milk, ½ cup
- Cayenne pepper, 1 teaspoon
- Fresh lemon juice, 1 tablespoon
- Garlic, 1 teaspoon, minced
- Cilantro, freshly chopped for topping
- Brown sugar, 1 teaspoon

1. In a skillet, combine all the ingredients, except the mussels.
2. Heat the mixture and bring it to a boil.
3. Add the mussels, and cook for 10 min.
4. Serve in a dish with the boiled liquid.

Per Serving:

Calories: 483; Fat: 24.4g; Carbs: 21.6g; Protein: 49g

Hot And Fresh Fishy Steaks
Preparation Time: 14 minutes
Cooking Time: 14 minutes
Total Time: 28 minutes

- Garlic, 1 clove, minced
- Lemon juice, 1 tbsp
- Brown sugar, 1 tbsp
- Halibut steak, 1 pound
- Salt and pepper to taste
- Soy sauce, ¼ tsp
- Butter, 1 tsp
- Greek yogurt, 2 tbsp

1. Over a medium flame, preheat the grill.
2. Mix the butter, sugar, yogurt, lemon juice, soy sauce and seasonings in a bowl.
3. Warm the mixture in a pan.
4. Use this mixture to brush onto the steak while cooking on the griller.
5. Serve hot.

Per Serving:
Calories: 412, Fat: 19.4g, Carbs: 35.6g, Protein: 25.7g

Garlic & Lemon Sea Bass

Preparation Time: 10 minutes
Cooking Time: 15 minutes
Total Time: 25 minutes

- 2 tbsp olive oil
- 2 sea bass fillets
- 1 lemon, juiced
- 4 garlic cloves, minced
- Salt and black pepper to taste

1. Preheat the oven to 380F. Line a baking sheet with parchment paper. Brush sea bass fillets with lemon juice, olive oil, garlic, salt, pepper and arrange them on the sheet.
2. Bake for 15 minutes. Serve with salad.

Per Serving:
Calories: 530, Fat: 30g, Carbs: 15g, Protein: 54g

- ½ cup quinoa
- 1 lemon, cut in wedges, to garnish
- 6 tiger shrimp, peeled and cooked
- ¼ cup olive oil
- 1 tomato, sliced
- 1 bell pepper, thinly sliced
- ½ cup black olives pitted and halved
- ½ red onion, chopped
- ½ tsp dried dill
- 1 tbsp fresh parsley, chopped
- Salt and black pepper to taste

1. In a pot place the quinoa and cover with 1 cup of water over medium heat. Bring boiling, reduce the heat, and simmer for 12-15 minutes or until tender.
2. Remove from heat and fluff it with a fork. Mix the quinoa with olive oil, dill, parsley, salt, and black pepper. Stir in tomatoes, bell peppers, olives, and onion.
3. Serve decorated with shrimp and lemon wedges.

Per Serving:
Calories: 662, Fat: 20.9g, Carbs: 37.8g, Protein: 78.8g

Lemony Shrimp & Quinoa Bowl

Preparation Time: 15 minutes
Cooking Time: 20 minutes
Total Time: 35 minutes

Sicilian Olive Chicken

Preparation Time: 10 minutes
Cooking Time: 15 minutes
Total Time: 25 minutes

- chicken cutlets, each about 4-ounce
- ¼ teaspoon crushed red pepper
- 7-ounce cherry tomatoes halved
- ½ tablespoon capers, rinsed
- ¼ cup Sicilian olive halves
- ¼ teaspoon ground black pepper
- ¾ cup chopped spinach, thawed if frozen
- ½ tablespoon olive oil

1. Take a large bowl, place tomatoes, olive, spinach, capers and red pepper. Stir until well mixed.
2. Place the chicken cutlets on a cutting board, and then season with black pepper until coated.
3. Take a medium skillet pan, place it over medium-high heat, add oil, and when hot, add the prepared chicken cutlets and then cook for 4 to 5 minutes per side until nicely brown.
4. Add the prepared tomato mixture to the pan, switch heat to medium level, cover the pan with its lid and then cook for 5 minutes until the chicken has thoroughly cooked.
5. When done, place the chicken on a serving plate, add the tomato mixture on the side, and serve.

Per Serving
Calories: 213; Fat: 8.4g; Sat. Fat: 1.5g; Carbs: 9.3g; Protein: 26.1g

Lemon Soup With Chicken

Preparation Time: 10 minutes
Cooking Time: 25 minutes
Total Time: 35 minutes

- 1 large leg of chicken
- 1 medium shallots, peeled, minced
- 1 large carrot, peeled, sliced
- 1 clove of garlic, peeled
- 1 big celery rib, cut into 4 pieces
- ¼ teaspoon, ground black pepper
- ¼ cup thyme leaves, fresh
- ¼ teaspoon salt, divided
- ¼ cup dill, chopped
- ½ tablespoon Acini di pepe
- 2 large egg yolks
- 1 tablespoon lemon juice
- ½ tablespoon olive oil
- 4 cups of water

1. Place the chicken on a cutting board, and then season with salt and black pepper until coated.
2. Take a large saucepan, place it over medium heat, add oil, and when hot, add the prepared chicken leg, cook for 5 minutes per side or until golden and then transfer to a cutting board.
3. Add shallots and garlic into the pan, stir in salt, cook for 2 minutes until softened, add carrots and celery, and cook for 3 minutes.

4 Add dill, and thyme, cook for 1 minute, return chicken into the pan, pour in the water and then cook for 30 minutes or more until chicken turns soft.

5 When done, remove the chicken leg from the pan, discard the bones, shred the chicken, and set it aside.

6 Remove celery, dill, and thyme from the saucepan, add acini di pepe, switch heat to the high level, and cook for 5 to 10 minutes until vegetables turn tender.

7 Take a small bowl, add egg yolks, add ½ cup of the soup mixture into the bowl, and whisk until combined.

8 Switch heat to medium level, add shredded chicken and cook for 3 to 5 minutes until thoroughly warmed.

9 Turn off the heat, continuously stir the egg yolks mixture until well combined, and then stir in lemon juice until mixed.

10 Ladle the soup evenly between two bowls and then serve.

Per Serving
Calories: 252.8; Fat: 8g; Sat. Fat: 1.8g; Carbs: 19.8g; Protein: 25.6g

Chicken Skillet With Mushrooms
Preparation Time: 5 minutes
Cooking Time: 15 minutes
Total Time: 20 minutes

- 5-ounce portobello mushrooms, sliced
- ½ of a large white onion, peeled, cut into round slices
- 1-pound chicken breast, cut into strips
- ¼ teaspoon salt, divided
- ¼ teaspoon ground black pepper, divided
- ½ teaspoon dried thyme
- 1 ½ tablespoon olive oil, divided
- ½ tablespoon balsamic vinegar
- 3 tablespoons white wine
- ¼ cup vegetable broth
- 1-ounce parmesan cheese, sliced

1 Take a large bowl, place chicken strips in it, add salt, black pepper, and thyme, pour in oil, vinegar, and white wine, toss until well coated, and set aside until required.

2 Take a medium skillet pan, place it over medium heat, add oil, and when hot, add onion and cook for 1 minute until begin to tender.

3 Add mushroom, salt, and black pepper, pour in the vegetable broth, cook for 5 minutes until softened, and when done, transfer the mushroom mixture into a bowl.

4 Then add marinated chicken into the pan, cook for 5 minutes, return the mushroom mixture into the pan, and cook for 3 minutes until thoroughly hot.

5 When done, place the cooked mushroom chicken into a serving plate, place parmesan slices on the side, and serve.

Per Serving
Calories: 245; Fat: 9.5g; Sat. Fat: 4.1g; Carbs: 8.5g; Protein: 31g

Saffron Chicken Thighs And Green Beans

Preparation Time: 10 minutes
Cooking Time: 25 minutes
Total Time: 35 minutes

- 1-pound chicken thighs, boneless and skinless
- 1 teaspoon saffron powder
- 1-pound green beans, trimmed and halved
- ½ cup Greek yogurt
- Salt and black pepper to taste
- 1 tablespoon lime juice
- 1 tablespoon dill, chopped

1 In a roasting pan, combine the chicken with the saffron, green beans and the rest of the ingredients, toss a bit, introduce in the oven and bake at 400 degrees F for 25 minutes.
2 Divide everything between plates and serve.

Per Serving:
Calories: 274, fat: 12.3g, carbs: 20.4g, protein: 14.3g

Almond-Crusted Chicken Tenders With Honey

Preparation Time: 10 minutes
Cooking Time: 20 minutes
Total Time: 30 minutes

- 1 tablespoon honey
- 1 tablespoon whole-grain or Dijon mustard
- ¼ teaspoon freshly ground black pepper
- ¼ teaspoon kosher or sea salt
- 1-pound skinless, boneless chicken breast tenders or tenderloins
- 1 cup almonds, roughly chopped
- Nonstick cooking spray

1 Preheat the oven to 425F. Cover a large pan with parchment paper.
2 Place a wire cooling rack on the parchment-lined baking sheet, and spray the rack well with nonstick cooking spray.
3 Combine the pepper, honey, mustard, and salt in a large bowl. Add the chicken and toss gently to coat. Set aside.
4 Dump the almonds onto a large sheet of parchment paper and spread them out. Press the coated chicken tenders into the nuts until evenly coated on all sides.
5 Place the chicken on the rack. Bake in the oven for 20-22 minutes, or until the internal temperature of the chicken measures 165ºF (74ºC) on a meat thermometer and any juices run clear.
6 Cool for 5 minutes before serving.

Per Serving

Calories: 222; fat: 7.0g; protein: 11.0g; carbs: 29.0g;

Grilled Chicken Breasts With Spinach Pesto

Preparation Time: 10 minutes
Cooking Time: 15 minutes
Total Time: 25 minutes

- 2 boneless, skinless chicken breasts
- ¼ cup + 1 tbsp olive oil
- 1/2 cup spinach
- ¼ cup grated Pecorino cheese
- Salt and black pepper to taste
- ¼ cup pine nuts
- 1 garlic clove, minced

1 Rub chicken with salt and black pepper. Grease a grill pan with 1 tbsp of olive oil and place over medium heat. Grill the chicken for 8-10 minutes, flipping once. Mix spinach, garlic, Pecorino cheese, and pine nuts in a food processor.
2 Slowly, pour in the remaining oil; pulse until smooth. Spoon 1 tbsp of pesto on each breast and cook for an additional 5 minutes.

Per Serving:

Calories: 493, Fat: 27g, Carbs: 4g, Protein: 53g

Italian Chicken

Preparation Time: 10 minutes
Cooking Time: 20 minutes
Total Time: 30 minutes

- 2 chicken breast halves
- 1/2 onion, chopped
- 1 green bell pepper, chopped
- 1 garlic clove, minced
- ½ cup Marsala wine
- 1 (14-oz) can crushed tomatoes
- 1 (14-oz) can white beans, drained
- 1 tbsp Italian seasoning
- 1/2 cup baby spinach
- ⅛ tsp red pepper flakes
- 2 tbsp olive oil
- Salt and black pepper to taste

1 Pound the chicken to ¾-inch thickness using a meat mallet. Warm the E.V.O. oil in a pan over medium heat and brown the chicken for 6 min. on both sides; set aside. In the same pan, sauté the onion, garlic, and bell pepper for 5 minutes.
2 Pour in the wine and scrape any bits from the bottom. Simmer for 1 minute. Stir in tomatoes, beans, Italian seasoning, salt, pepper, and pepper flakes. Boiling, then lower the heat and gently simmer for 5 minutes.
3 Stir in spinach and put back the reserved chicken; cook for 3-4 more minutes. Serve and enjoy.

Per Serving:

Calories: 605, Fat: 11.5g, Carb: 74.2g, Protein: 47.8g

Spiced Chicken Meatballs

Preparation Time: 10 minutes
Cooking Time: 20 minutes
Servings: 2

- 0.5-pound chicken meat, ground
- 1/2 tablespoon pine nuts, toasted and chopped
- 1 egg, whisked
- 1 teaspoon turmeric powder
- 1 garlic clove, minced
- Salt and black pepper to taste
- 1 cup heavy cream
- 1 tablespoon olive oil
- ¼ cup parsley, chopped
- 1 tablespoon chives, chopped

1. In a bowl, combine the pine nuts with the chicken and the rest of the ingredients except the oil and the cream; stir well and shape medium meatballs out of this mix.
2. Heat a pan with the oil over medium-high heat, add the meatballs and cook them for 4 minutes on each side.
3. Add the cream, toss gently, cook everything over medium heat for 10 minutes more, divide between plates and serve.

Per Serving:
Calories: 283, fat: 9.2, carbs: 24.4, protein: 34.5

Lemony Turkey And Pine Nuts

Preparation Time: 10 minutes
Cooking Time: 25 minutes
Total Time: 35 minutes

- 1 turkey breast, boneless, skinless and halved
- A pinch of salt and black pepper
- 1 tablespoon avocado oil
- Juice of 1 lemon
- 1 tablespoon rosemary, chopped
- 2 garlic cloves, minced
- ¼ cup pine nuts, chopped
- 1 cup chicken stock

1. Heat a pan with the oil over medium-high heat, add the garlic and the turkey and brown for 4 minutes on each side.
2. Add the rest of the ingredients, bring to a simmer and cook over medium heat for 20 minutes.
3. Divide the mix between plates and serve with a side salad.

Per Serving:
Calories: 293, fat: 12.4, carbs: 17.8, protein 34

Vegetable & Chicken Skewers

Preparation Time: 10 minutes
Cooking Time: 15 minutes
Total Time: 25 minutes

- 2 tbsp olive oil
- 1 chicken breast, cubed
- 1/2 red bell pepper, cut into squares
- 1/2 red onion, cut into squares
- 1/2 cup mushrooms, quartered
- 1 tsp sweet paprika
- 1 tsp ground nutmeg
- 1 tsp Italian seasoning
- ¼ tsp smoked paprika
- Salt and black pepper to taste
- ¼ tsp ground cardamom
- 1 lemon, juiced
- 2 garlic cloves, minced

1 Combine chicken, onion, bell pepper, paprika, nutmeg, Italian seasoning, paprika, salt, pepper, cardamom, lemon juice, garlic, and olive oil in a bowl. Transfer to the fridge covered for 30 minutes. Preheat your grill to high. Alternate chicken cubes, peppers, mushrooms, and onions on each of 4 metal skewers.
2 Grill them for 16 minutes on all sides, turning frequently. Serve with salad.

Per Serving:
Calories: 270, Fat: 15g, Carbs: 15g, Protein: 21g

Tuscan Style Chicken

Preparation Time: 10 minutes
Cooking Time: 10 minutes
Total Time: 20 minutes

- 5 oz chicken breast, skinless, boneless, roughly chopped
- 1 tablespoon olive oil
- ½ cup organic almond milk
- 1 oz Parmesan, grated
- ½ teaspoon chili flakes
- ¼ teaspoon ground nutmeg

1. Heat the olive oil, add chicken breast, and sprinkle with chili flakes.
2. Roast the chicken for 3 minutes and stir.
3. Then add almond milk, ground nutmeg, and Parmesan.
4. Close the lid and simmer the chicken for 20 minutes on low heat.

Per Serving
Calories: 270; Fat: 13g; Carbs: 20g; Protein: 17g

BEEF PORK AND LAMB

Hamburgers

Preparation Time: 10 minutes
Cooking Time: 10 minutes
Total Time: 20 minutes

- 1-pound ground beef, extra-lean
- ¼ teaspoon garlic powder
- ¼ cup chopped roasted red bell pepper, divided
- ½ teaspoon salt
- ¼ cup sliced onion
- ¼ teaspoon ground black pepper
- ¼ cup arugula leaves, fresh
- ½ teaspoon ground cumin
- 2 tablespoons chopped parsley, fresh
- ¼ teaspoon ground oregano
- ¼ teaspoon paprika
- 2 whole-wheat hamburger buns
- 2 tablespoons crumbled feta cheese, low fat

1 Take a griddle pan greased with oil, place it over medium-high heat and let it preheat.
2 Meanwhile, take a large bowl, add beef, bell pepper, cumin, oregano, paprika, garlic powder, black pepper, parsley, and salt, stir until well combined, and then shape the mixture into 2 patties.
3 Place the prepared patties on the griddle pan, and then cook for 5 minutes per side until thoroughly cooked and brown.
4 Then place hamburgers on the griddle pan, grill for a minute until hot and toasted, and place them on a plate.

5 Assemble the hamburger and for this, place bell pepper, onion, arugula, and feta cheese on the bottom slice of the bun and then top with the cooked patty.
6 Cover with the top side of the bun and then serve.

Per Serving
Calories: 270; Fat: 13g; Sat. Fat: 5g; Carbs: 20g; Protein: 17g

---

Spiced Lamb And Beef Kebabs

Preparation Time: 15 minutes
Cooking Time: 20 minutes
Total Time: 35 minutes

- ¼ pound ground beef
- 1 tablespoon cilantro leaves
- ½ cup diced white onion
- ¼ pound ground lamb
- ½ teaspoon ground coriander
- 2 teaspoon minced Thai chilies
- ¼ cup chickpea flour
- 1 teaspoon minced garlic
- ½ inch of ginger, peeled, grated
- ½ teaspoon dried mint
- ¼ teaspoon salt
- ¼ teaspoon cayenne pepper
- ¼ teaspoon ground cinnamon
- ½ teaspoon lemon zest
- ¼ teaspoon dried dill
- 1 teaspoon lime juice
- 1 tablespoon olive oil
- 1 large egg, at room temperature

1. Take a large bowl, crack the egg in it, add beef, lamb, salt, cayenne, cinnamon, coriander, garlic, and Thai chili, and stir until well combined.
2. Then add lime juice, lemon zest, mint, onion, flour, dill, and ginger, stir until well mixed and shape into evenly sized small patties.
3. Take a large skillet pan, place it over medium-high heat, add oil, and when hot, place the prepared patties into the pan and then cook for 4 minutes per side until thoroughly cooked and golden brown.
4. Sprinkle cilantro on top of the patties, and then serve.

Per Serving
Calories: 217; Fat: 15.4g; Sat. Fat: 7g; Carbs: 2.8g; Protein: 18g

---

Herb Crusted Pork Tenderloin

Preparation Time: 10 minutes
Cooking Time: 20 minutes
Total Time: 30 minutes

- ½ pound pork lion
- 1 teaspoon dried oregano
- ¼ teaspoon lemon-pepper seasoning
- 1 teaspoon olive oil
- 3 teaspoons olive tapenade
- 3 teaspoons crumbled feta cheese, low-fat

1. Place the tenderloin on a cutting board, brush with oil, sprinkle with lemon-pepper seasoning and oregano until well coated.

2. Then wrap the prepared tenderloin with plastic wrap, place it in the refrigerator and then let it rest for 1 hour.
3. When ready to cook, set a grill greased with oil, set it to a medium-high heat setting, and let it preheat.
4. Then place the tenderloin on a cutting board, unwrap it, and make a lengthwise cut on the pork, not letting it cut through.
5. Open the cut in the pork, spread olive tapenade on one side, sprinkle with feta cheese, close the cut with a twine string tying two times, forming its original form.
6. Place the prepared tenderloin on the grill, cook for 20 minutes, or until thoroughly cooked, and then transfer the tenderloin to a cutting board.
7. Cover the pork loosely with foil, let it rest for 10 minutes, then cut into slices and then serve.

Per Serving
Calories: 209; Fat: 10.3g; Sat. Fat: 2.3g; Carbs: 0.6g; Protein: 26.8g

---

Sage Pork Chops With Sweet & Spicy Chutney

Preparation Time: 10 minutes
Cooking Time: 25 minutes
Total Time: 35 minutes

- 1 tbsp olive oil
- ½ tsp garlic powder
- 2 pork loin chops, boneless

- Salt and black pepper to taste
- ¼ tsp ground cumin
- ½ tsp sage, dried
- 1 tsp chili powder

For the chutney:
- ¼ cup shallot, minced
- 1 tsp olive oil
- 2 cups apricots, peeled and chopped
- ½ cup red sweet pepper, chopped
- ½ jalapeno pepper, minced
- 1 tbsp balsamic vinegar
- 2 tbsp cilantro, chopped

1. Warm the olive oil in a skillet over medium heat and cook the shallot for 5 minutes. Stir in sweet pepper, apricots, jalapeño pepper, vinegar, and cilantro and cook for 10 minutes. Remove from heat.
2. In the meantime, sprinkle pork chops with olive oil, salt, pepper, garlic powder, cumin, sage, and chili powder.
3. Preheat the grill to medium heat. Grill pork chops for 12-14 minutes on both sides. Serve topped with apricot chutney.

Per Serving:
Calories: 300, Fat: 11g, Carbs: 14g, Protein: 39g

- 0.5-pound ground lamb
- ½ teaspoon salt
- ½ teaspoon freshly ground black pepper
- 1 tablespoon crumbled feta cheese
- Buns, toppings, and tzatziki, for serving (optional)

1. Preheat the grill to high heat. In a wide bowl, stir the lamb with salt and pepper using your hands.
2. Divide the meat into 2 portions. Divide each portion in half to make a top and a bottom. Flatten each half into a 3-inch circle.
3. Make a dent in the center of one of the halves and place 1 tablespoon of feta cheese in the center.
4. Place the second half of the patty on top of the feta cheese and press down to close the 2 halves together, making it resemble a round burger.
5. Grill each side for 3 minutes, for medium-well.
6. If desired, serve on a bun with your favorite toppings and tzatziki sauce.

Per Serving
Calories: 345; fat: 29.0g; protein: 20.0g; carbs: 1.0g

Greek-Style Lamb Burgers
Preparation Time: 10 minutes
Cooking Time: 10 minutes
Total Time: 20 minutes

Easy Pork Chops In Tomato Sauce
Preparation Time: 10 minutes
Cooking Time: 10 minutes
Total Time: 20 minutes

- 2 tbsp olive oil
- 2 pork loin chops, boneless
- 3 tomatoes, peeled and crushed
- 2 tbsp basil, chopped
- ¼ cup black olives pitted and halved
- 1/2 yellow onion, chopped
- 1 garlic clove, minced

1. Warm the olive oil in a skillet over medium heat and brown pork chops for 6 minutes on all sides. Share into plates.
2. In the same skillet, stir tomatoes, basil, olives, onion, and garlic and simmer for 4 minutes. Drizzle tomato sauce over pork to serve.

Per Serving:
Calories: 340, Fat: 18g, Carbs: 13g, Protein: 35g

Lamb Chops

Preparation Time: 10 minutes
Cooking Time: 8 minutes
Total Time: 18 minutes

- 4 lamb chops
- 3-ounce arugula leaves, fresh
- ½ medium fennel bulb, halved, sliced
- ¼ teaspoon salt, divided
- 1 tablespoon oregano leaves, fresh
- ½ teaspoon chopped garlic
- ¼ teaspoon ground black pepper, divided
- 2 medium tomatoes, sliced
- 3 teaspoons olive oil
- 2 teaspoons lemon juice

1. Switch on the oven, set the temperature to 205 degrees C or 400 degrees F, and preheat.
2. Meanwhile, take a baking tray, line it with parchment paper, and set it aside until required.
3. Place the lamb chops on a cutting board and then season with salt and black pepper until coated.
4. Take a large skillet pan, place it over medium-high heat, add oil and when hot, place the lamb chops and then cook for 4 minutes per side or until golden.
5. Transfer the lamb chops onto the prepared baking tray and bake for 8 minutes or thoroughly cooked.
6. Meanwhile, take a medium bowl, add tomatoes, oregano, garlic, fennel, lemon juice, oil, salt, and black pepper, and stir until combined.
7. When done, place the lamb chops on a serving plate, add arugula leaves on the side, and spoon the prepared tomato mixture over the arugula and serve.

Per Serving
Calories: 232; Fat: 12g; Sat. Fat: 2.2g; Carbs: 6.8g; Protein: 24.5g

Lamb Pita With Tzatziki Sauce

Preparation Time: 15 minutes
Cooking Time: 20 minutes
Total Time: 35 minutes

- ½ pound ground lamb
- ¼ cup chopped cucumber, divided
- 3 teaspoons minced garlic
- ¼ teaspoon salt, divided
- 4 tablespoons chopped white onion
- ¼ teaspoon ground black pepper
- ¼ cup grape tomatoes, halved
- ¼ teaspoon ground cumin
- 1 cup chopped lettuce
- ¼ teaspoon cayenne pepper
- 1 tablespoon chopped parsley, fresh
- 1 teaspoon chopped dill, fresh
- 1 teaspoon lemon zest
- 2 whole-grain pita pockets, warmed
- ½ teaspoon red wine vinegar
- 3 ounces yogurt, low-fat

1. Switch on the oven, set the temperature to 205 degrees C or 400 degrees F, and preheat.
2. Meanwhile, take a baking tray, line it with a parchment sheet, and set it aside until required.
3. Take a small bowl, add yogurt, cucumber, dill, vinegar, and salt, stir until combined, and set it aside until required.
4. Take a large bowl, place the lamb, garlic, parsley, lemon zest, salt, black pepper, and cayenne pepper in it, and stir until combined.
5. Shape the mixture into evenly sized meatballs, arrange them on the prepared baking tray and then bake for 20 minutes until thoroughly cooked and nicely browned, flipping halfway.
6. Assemble the pita, and for this, place pita bread, layer with half of each of lettuce, cucumber, tomatoes, and drizzle the yogurt mixture over the vegetables.
7. Place meatballs on pita bread, prepare the other pita in the same manner and serve.

Per Serving
Calories: 307; Fat: 7.2g; Sat. Fat: 2.2g; Carbs: 26.1g; Protein: 33.3g

Lamb Meatballs With Tzatziki
Preparation Time: 15 minutes
Cooking Time: 18 minutes
Total Time: 33 minutes

- ½ pound ground lamb
- ¼ teaspoon minced garlic
- ½ teaspoon salt
- 3 teaspoon pork rinds, blended
- 3 tablespoon chopped parsley, fresh
- 1 teaspoon ground cumin
- ¼ teaspoon ground black pepper
- ½ tablespoon chopped dill, fresh
- ½ teaspoon ground coriander
- 1 tablespoon olive oil
- ½ cup tzatziki sauce
- 1 large egg, at room temperature

1. Switch on the oven, set the temperature to 205 degrees C or 400 degrees F, and preheat.
2. Meanwhile, take a baking tray, line it with parchment paper, and set it aside until required.
3. Take a large bowl, crack the egg in it, add lamb, pork rinds, parsley, oregano, cumin, coriander, garlic, black pepper, and salt, and stir until combined.
4. Shape the mixture into evenly sized meatballs, arrange them on the prepared

baking tray and then bake for 20 minutes until thoroughly cooked.

5   When done, place the meatballs on a serving plate, and then serve with tzatziki sauce.

Per Serving
Calories: 212; Fat: 14.2g; Sat. Fat: 5.7g; Carbs: 2.8g; Protein: 18.3g

Basil Meatballs

Preparation Time: 15 minutes
Cooking Time: 10 minutes
Total Time: 25 minutes

- 5 oz ground pork
- 1 teaspoon dried basil
- ½ teaspoon chili flakes
- 2 tablespoons water
- 1 teaspoon ground paprika
- 1 tablespoon olive oil

1. Mix ground pork with basil, chili flakes, water, and ground paprika.
2. After this, make the small meatballs.
3. Preheat the olive oil in the skillet.
4. Add the meatballs in the hot oil and roast for 4 minutes per side.

Per Serving:
Calories: 133; Fat: 6g; Carbs: 2.5g; Protein: 18.6g

Tomato Meat Mince

Preparation Time: 10 minutes
Cooking Time: 20 minutes
Total Time: 30 minutes

- 1 cup ground beef
- 2 tomatoes, chopped
- 1 teaspoon fresh basil, chopped
- 1 garlic clove, diced
- 1 tablespoon olive oil

1. Heat olive oil in the skillet.
2. Add ground beef and roast it for 5 minutes.
3. Then sprinkle the meat with basil, tomatoes, and garlic clove.
4. Stir the ground meat mixture well and cook with the closed lid for 15 minutes.

Per Serving:
Calories: 107; Fat: 7.7g; Carbs: 2.7g; Protein: 7.1g

Thyme Pork Steak

Preparation Time: 10 minutes
Cooking Time: 10 minutes
Total Time: 20 minutes

- 2 pork steaks
- 1 tablespoon dried thyme
- 1 tablespoon balsamic vinegar
- 1 tablespoon olive oil

1. Rub the meat with dried thyme and brush with balsamic vinegar and olive oil.
2. Leave the meat for 15 minutes to marinate.
3. After this, preheat the skillet until hot.
4. Put the steaks in the hot skillet and roast for 6 minutes per side.

Per Serving:
Calories: 285; Fat: 21g; Carbs: 0.9g; Protein: 21.9g

---

4. Cook the tender medallions for 15 minutes on medium heat.

Per Serving:
Calories: 180; Fat: 7.2g; Carbs: 2.9g; Protein: 24g

Tender Medallions

Preparation Time: 20 minutes
Cooking Time: 23 minutes
Total Time: 43 minutes

- 6 oz pork tenderloin
- 1 teaspoon olive oil
- ¼ cup plain yogurt
- 1 teaspoon curry paste

1. Cut the pork tenderloin into 2 servings and roast in the olive oil for 3 minutes per side.
2. Meanwhile, whisk the curry powder with plain yogurt.
3. Pour the yogurt mixture over the meat, coat it well, and close the lid.

DESSERT

Spicy Hot Chocolate

Preparation Time: 10 minutes
Cooking Time: 10 minutes
Total Time: 20 minutes

- ¼ tsp cayenne pepper powder
- 2 squares semisweet chocolate
- 2 cups milk
- 1 tsp sugar
- ¼ tsp ground cinnamon
- ¼ tsp salt

1. Place milk and sugar in a pot over low heat and warm until it simmers. Combine dark chocolate, cinnamon, salt, and cayenne pepper powder in a bowl. Slowly pour in enough hot milk to cover.
2. Return the pot to the heat and lower the temperature. Mix until the chocolate has melted, then combine the remaining milk. Spoon into 2 cups and serve hot.

Per Serving:
Calories: 342, Fat: 23g, Carbs: 22g, Protein: 12g

Baked Apples With Cardamom Sauce

Preparation Time: 10 minutes
Cooking Time: 20 minutes
Total Time: 30 minutes

- 1 ½ tsp cardamom
- 1 tsp olive oil
- ½ tsp salt
- 4 firm apples, peeled, cored, and sliced
- 2 tbsp honey
- 2 tbsp milk

1. Preheat oven to 390°F. In a bowl, combine apple slices, salt and half tsp of the cardamom. Place them on a greased pan dish and cook for 20 minutes. Remove to a serving plate. In the meantime, place milk, honey, and remaining cardamom in a pot over medium heat.
2. Cook until simmer. Drop the sauce over the apples and serve immediately.

Per Serving:
Calories: 287, Fat: 3g, Carbs: 69g, Protein: 2g

Fruit Cups With Orange Juice

Preparation Time: 10 minutes
Cooking Time: 0 minutes
Total Time: 10 minutes

- 1 cup orange juice
- ½ cup watermelon cubes
- 1 ½ cups grapes, halved
- 1 cup chopped cantaloupe
- ½ cup cherries, pitted and chopped
- 1 peach, chopped
- ½ tsp ground cinnamon

1 Combine watermelon cubes, grapes, cherries, cantaloupe, and peach in a bowl. Add the juice of an orange and mix well.
2 Share into dessert cups, dust with cinnamon, and serve chilled.

Per Serving:
Calories: 156, Fat: 0.5g, Carbs: 24.2g, Protein: 1.8g

Strawberry & Cocoa Yogurt

Preparation Time: 5 minutes
Cooking Time: 0 minutes
Total Time: 5 minutes

- ¾ cup Greek yogurt
- 1 tbsp cocoa powder
- ¼ cup strawberries, chopped
- 5 drops vanilla stevia

1 Combine cocoa powder, strawberries, yogurt, and stevia in a bowl. Serve immediately.

Per Serving:
Calories: 210, Fat: 9g, Carbs: 8g, Protein: 5g

Raspberries & Lime Frozen Yogurt

Preparation Time: 10 minutes
Cooking Time: 0 minutes
Total Time: 10 minutes

- 1 cup fresh raspberries
- 2 cups vanilla frozen yogurt
- 1 lime, zested
- ¼ cup chopped praline pecans

1 Divide the frozen yogurt into 4 dessert glasses. Top with raspberries, lime zest, and pecans. Serve immediately.

Per Serving:
Calories: 142, Fat: 3.4g, Carbs: 26.2g, Protein: 3.7g

Melon Cucumber Smoothie

Preparation Time: 30 minutes
Cooking Time: 0 minutes
Total Time: 30 minutes

- ½ cucumber
- 2 slices of melon
- 2 tablespoons lemon juice
- 1 pear, peeled and sliced
- 3 fresh mint leaves
- ½ cup almond milk

1   Place all ingredients in a blender. Blend until smooth. Pour into a glass vessel and let cool in the refrigerator for at least 30 minutes.

Per Serving:
Calories: 253; Carbs: 59.3g; Protein: 5.7g; Fat: 2.1g

Maple Grilled Pineapple

Preparation Time: 5 minutes
Cooking Time: 10 minutes
Total Time: 15 minutes

- 1 tbsp maple syrup
- 1 pineapple, peeled and cut into wedges
- ½ tsp ground cinnamon

1. Preheat a grill pan over high heat. Drizzle the fruit in a bowl with maple syrup; sprinkle with ground cinnamon.
2. Grill for about 7-8 minutes, occasionally turning until the fruit chars slightly. Serve.

Per Serving:
Calories: 120, Fat: 1g, Carbs: 33g, Protein: 1g

Honey Berry Granita

Preparation Time: 30 minutes
Cooking Time: 0 minutes
Total Time: 30 minutes

- 1 tsp lemon juice
- ¼ cup honey
- 1 cup fresh strawberries
- 1 cup fresh raspberries
- 1 cup fresh blueberries

1. Bring 2-cup of water to a boil in a pot over high heat. Stir in honey until dissolved. Remove from the heat and mix in berries and lemon juice; let cool.

2. Once cooled, add the mixture to a food processor and pulse until smooth. Transfer to a shallow glass and freeze for 1 hour. Stir with a fork and freeze for 30 more minutes.
3. Repeat a couple of times. Serve in dessert dishes.

Per Serving:
Calories: 115, Fat: 1g, Carbs: 29g, Protein: 1g

Yogurt And Berry Tiramisu
Preparation Time: 15 minutes
Cooking Time: 5 minutes
Total Time: 20 minutes

- ¾ cup desired berries, fresh
- 4 small sponge cupcakes, vanilla flavored, low-fat
- 1 tablespoon brown sugar
- 3 tablespoon cocoa powder, unsweetened
- ½ teaspoon vanilla extract, unsweetened
- 1 cup yogurt, low-fat
- 2 tablespoon blueberry juice, unsweetened
- ¼ cup water

1 Take a small pot, place it over low heat, add ¼ cup berries and sugar, pour in the water, and then cook for 5 minutes or more until the sugar has melted.
2 Then remove the pot from heat and let it cool at room temperature.
3 Take a large bowl, place yogurt in it, vanilla extract, and stir until well blended.

4 Take a serving glass, place two cupcakes in it and then top with one-fourth of the prepared berry mixture.
5 Layer the berry mixture with the prepared yogurt mixture, sprinkle with half of the cocoa powder, and then layer it with one-fourth of the prepared berry mixture.
6 Assemble another parfait glass in the same manner and then serve.

Per Serving
Calories: 220; Fat: 1g; Sat. Fat: 0.2g; Carbs: 41.3g; Protein: 4g

Blueberry Muffins
Preparation Time: 10 minutes
Cooking Time: 15 minutes
Total Time: 25 minutes

- ½ cup blueberries, fresh or thawed if frozen
- ½ cup whole-wheat flour
- ½ cup all-purpose flour
- 4 tablespoons sugar
- ¼ teaspoon salt
- 1 ½ teaspoon baking powder
- 4 tablespoons olive oil
- 1 small egg, at room temperature
- ½ cup almond milk, low-fat, unsweetened

1 Switch on the oven, set the temperature to 204 degrees C or 400 degrees F, and preheat.

2   Meanwhile, four silicone muffin cups, grease them with oil, and set them aside until required.

3   Take a medium bowl, add flours, add baking powder, salt, and sugar, stir until well combined, and fold in blueberries until well incorporated.

4   Take a small bowl, crack the egg, pour in milk and oil, and stir until well mixed.

5   Stir the prepared egg mixture into the prepared flour mixture, stir until well combined, and then divide the mixture evenly among the prepared muffin cups, filling each three-fourths full.

6   Place the prepared muffin cups in the oven, bake for 15 to 18 minutes until firm, and the top turn golden, and then let them rest for 10 minutes.

7   Serve straight away.

Per Serving
Calories: 161; Fat: 4.6g; Sat. Fat: 2.5g; Carbs: 27.4g; Protein: 3.6g

---

1.   Place all ingredients in a mixing bowl. Toss to combine. Allow chilling in the fridge before serving.

Per Serving:
Calories: 107; Carbs: 9.9g; Protein: 1.6g; Fat: 7.8g

Strawberry And Avocado Medley

Preparation Time: 5 minutes
Cooking Time: 0 minutes
Total Time: 5 minutes

- 1 cup strawberry, halved
- 1/2 avocado, pitted and sliced
- 1 tablespoon slivered almonds

Cooking Measurement Chart

Weight

imperial	metric
1/2 oz	15 g
1 oz	29 g
2 oz	57 g
3 oz	85 g
4 oz	113 g
5 oz	141 g
6 oz	170 g
8 oz	227 g
10 oz	283 g
12 oz	340 g
13 oz	369 g
14 oz	397 g
15 oz	425 g
1 lb	453 g

Measurement

cup	onces	milliliters	tablespoons
8 cup	64 oz	1895 ml	128
6 cup	48 oz	1420 ml	96
5 cup	40 oz	1180 ml	80
4 cup	32 oz	960 ml	64
2 cup	16 oz	480 ml	32
1 cup	8 oz	240 ml	16
3/4 cup	6 oz	177 ml	12
2/3 cup	5 oz	158 ml	11
1/2 cup	4 oz	118 ml	8
3/8 cup	3 oz	90 ml	6
1/3 cup	2.5 oz	79 ml	5.5
1/4 cup	2 oz	59 ml	4
1/8 cup	1 oz	30 ml	3
1/16 cup	1/2 oz	15 ml	1

Temperature

fahrenheit	celsius
100 °F	37 °C
150 °F	65 °C
200 °F	93 °C
250 °F	121 °C
300 °F	150 °C
325 °F	160 °C
350 °F	180 °C
375 °F	190 °C
400 °F	200 °C
425 °F	220 °C
450 °F	230 °C
500 °F	260 °C
525 °F	274 °C
550 °F	288 °C

INDEX

NOTE

NOTE

Made in United States
Troutdale, OR
02/22/2024

17874798R00042